Manley War
Womens Re

Your Child's *Emotional* Needs

What they are and how to meet them

Dr Vicky Flory

FINCH PUBLISHING
SYDNEY

To all my family, friends and colleagues who believed in this book and my ability to write it – a very warm thank you!

Your Child's Emotional Needs
This edition first published in 2005 in Australia and New Zealand by Finch Publishing Pty Limited, PO Box 120, Lane Cove, NSW 1595, Australia. ABN 49 057 285 248

07 06 05   8 7 6 5 4 3 2 1

National Library of Australia Cataloguing-in-Publication entry
    Flory, Vicky.
    Your child's emotional needs: what they are and how to
    meet them.

    Includes index.
    ISBN 1 876451 65 3.

    1. Emotions in children. 2. Emotional problems of children.
    3. Child mental health. I. Title.
    155.4124

Edited by Colette Batha
Editorial assistance from Rosemary Peers
Text designed in Perpetua 12.5 / 15pt by Warren Ventures
Typesetting by J&M Typesetting
Cover design by Steve Miller – 154 Design
Cover photograph courtesy of Photolibrary.com
Printed by BPA Print Group

Photo credits   Zoe Finch, Rob Rathbone, Briony Timmins

Notes The 'Author's notes' section at the back of this book contains useful additional information and references to quoted material in the text. Each reference is linked to the text by its relevant page number and an identifying line entry.

Other Finch titles can be viewed at **www.finch.com.au**

Contents

Introduction

Parents instinctively know that emotions matter – they don't like to see their child unhappy – and one of their main aims is to raise a happy child who is able to cope with the challenges of life, has positive relationships with other people and a healthy self-esteem. Parents would agree that a healthy child is one who is emotionally well-adjusted. Nevertheless, many parents don't understand what their child's emotional needs are or what normal emotional development actually is. They may not be clear about how to respond to their child's tears and tantrums or how to understand their child's emotional health through the ups and downs of everyday life.

I find that parents are often very interested in these matters, but have heard very little about them compared with some of the more tangible, visible aspects of raising their children. Parents may have attended antenatal classes and parenting groups – but children's emotional needs are rarely the focus of such gatherings. This puts parents at a disadvantage, as they naturally need basic information about children's emotional development and needs if they are going to meet them.

This book outlines in simple, easy-to-understand terms children's emotional needs, how they are linked with children's behaviour, and how to meet those needs from birth to twelve years of age.

The key emotional needs that all children have are:

★ to have a secure relationship with a parent or other caregiver

★ to receive help with managing their emotions

★ to receive emotional support, particularly when they are experiencing difficulties

★ to have a sense of belonging

★ to feel loved

★ to feel accepted and approved of

★ to have clear expectations, routines and boundaries.

These points are discussed at greater length in Chapter 2.

I also examine some emotional difficulties that your child may face. Many people who have children with emotional difficulties do not seek professional help. They may think that their child will grow out of their problems, or that nothing can be done to help. While a book is not a substitute for professional assistance, it offers some pointers on how to recognise and manage the difficulties that are commonly experienced. If problems persist, it is important to seek professional assistance.

Your Child's Emotional Needs is suitable for people in various situations. You may simply want to gain a better understanding of your child's emotional development, in order to help him or her be as emotionally healthy as possible before reaching adolescence. Or you may feel that there is room for improvement in your relationship with your child – perhaps you feel frustrated with your child's tantrums and displays of emotion, and want to change unhealthy patterns of behaviour.

This book answers these questions:

★ How do we make sense of our children's emotions?

★ Are children's feelings just passing experiences that don't influence their development one way or another, or are they more central?

★ What is considered normal at different ages?

★ What can I do to help my child develop emotional health?

Part One explains the importance of children's emotions. It outlines what children's emotional needs are, why they are important and how children develop emotionally over time. I explain my theory of parental empathy and suggest processes that will help you meet your child's emotional needs. Part Two examines how children's emotional needs change over the first year of life, from ages one to four, and again from ages five to twelve. Part Three looks at childhood emotional disorders and common emotional difficulties, and ways you can help your child to deal with them.

WHY I WROTE IT

In my practice as a psychologist, I see many parents who are concerned about their child's behaviour and emotions. They often ask me where they can find more information about children's emotional needs, and as there didn't seem to be a book that deals specifically with these issues, I decided to fill that gap.

Essentially, my purpose is to bring parents closer to their children by helping them to understand the inner world of the child, to see why the child is behaving in a particular way, and to help the child develop healthy emotional habits for life.

I hope this book is useful and informative to parents and other carers of children.

Dr Vicky Flory BA (Hons) DPsych (MelbUni)
Psychologist

Note: In the interests of fairness, we use 'she' and 'he' in alternating chapters when talking about non-specific children.

PART ONE

UNDERSTANDING YOUR CHILD'S EMOTIONAL NEEDS

Why are children's emotions important?

Every parent has faced a situation like this:

An ill-timed tantrum

Tina is in a hurry to finish her shopping and only has one more shop to visit, but just when she needs her four-year-old son Paolo to cooperate, he throws a tantrum. He doesn't want to go any further, he screams, cries, and throws himself on the floor. Tina has mixed emotions – she's very annoyed, but also cringes as all shoppers' eyes focus on her and her screaming son.

Crying for no apparent reason

Jemima, ten months old, is crying. It's not clear why but she has been teary all day. Barry, her dad, has fed her and she's had her nap, but he can't get her interested in her toys. As soon as he walks away, she starts crying again. Barry feels frustrated. He's done all he can and is wondering whether he has spoilt Jemima by giving her too much attention in the past.

Reluctance to separate

Charlie, eighteen months old, cries bitterly when his mother Jenny drops him off at crèche. It wrenches her heart, but she has to go to work.

Ineffective reasoning with a child

Nada tries hard to be a good mum. She brings up her children by talking to them and explaining things. Her daughter Salma, six years old, still throws tantrums. Nada would have expected her to outgrow them by now. When Salma has to wait her turn for Nada's attention, or she thinks her sister Rana has been given more ice cream, she starts to cry loudly, becoming more and more upset until she has a full-blown tantrum. Nada doesn't want to reward tantrums so she ignores the drama and tells Salma she will talk to her when she is calmer. When Salma calms down, Nada explains the reasons she has to wait. She tells Salma that if she is upset about her serving of ice cream, all she has to do is say so and Nada will listen to her. Salma seems to understand this perfectly well. But next time there's a bit of tension, Salma throws another tantrum. Nada feels frustrated because it doesn't matter how much she reasons with Salma, her behaviour does not improve.

These are everyday examples of how children's emotions affect their behaviour. Of course, there are also positive emotions: children are exuberant about going fast on their new bike, picking flowers, patting a new puppy. It delights parents to see their child so enthusiastic about the world. At these moments, all seems right with their child – smiles and sunshine. But all too quickly something upsets their child: tears and tantrums disrupt the routine, escalate, and parents are left wondering what is the best way to respond (and maybe why their child can't stay happier for longer!).

Coping with children's negative emotions is high on the list of parents' daily challenges. Children can experience negative feelings frequently and intensely (hence the loud crying) and unpredictably (going from happy to downright furious in less than ten seconds!). This is especially true of children who are under five years of age. Parents are confronted with daily decisions about how to respond to their child's feelings. Should I ignore my child when she is carrying on so that she knows such behaviour won't be rewarded? If I spend too much time consoling my child, am I delaying her becoming independent?

There are three main reasons why you need to pay attention to your child's emotions:

UNDERSTANDING YOUR CHILD

To understand your child, you need to understand her emotions. Anyone's experience of life is greatly influenced by their emotional state, and this is also true for your child. If you don't know what your child is feeling, you are missing a big part of her experience.

Understanding your child's emotions

1. Where is my child in her emotional development?

2. How does my child feel at different times throughout the day?

3. What things upset my child?

4. What things make my child happy?

5. What does my child need from me to grow strong and healthy emotionally?

EMOTIONS DRIVE BEHAVIOUR

Children's emotions play a large role in their life, partly because emotions drive a lot of behaviour. We don't see children's emotions directly, but rather through their behaviour and facial expressions. This is true of adults as well. To some extent we may be able to tell how adults feel by how they behave. In adulthood the signs may be subtle, for example someone may become less talkative because their feelings have been hurt. People can learn to hide their feelings, but often facial expressions and some changes in behaviour will give them away. Children are more spontaneous. If your child is upset, you will probably know it pretty soon! She will cry, tantrum or pout. Her behaviour is obvious – her feelings less so. By considering your child's behaviour in the context of her feelings, you can understand her better.

Here is a diagram of how feelings and behaviour are related:

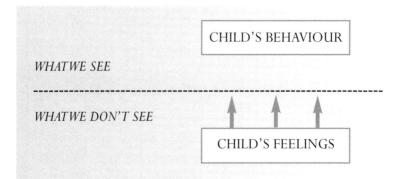

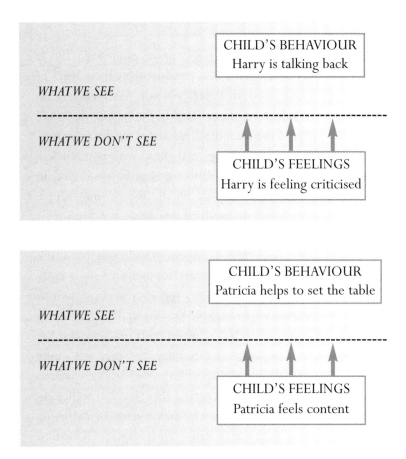

EMOTIONS AFFECT MANY PARTS OF A CHILD'S LIFE

Children's emotions affect their wellbeing, emotional intelligence, behaviour, self-esteem, social competence and school performance. Children's emotions impact on nearly every part of their life. So for you to understand what is going on for your child, and what she needs, you need to have an understanding of her emotions.

Wellbeing

Wellbeing is subjective. We might think someone's life is great, but only that person can comment on their level of wellbeing – how well they feel overall. Wellbeing is an important marker of emotional health. Someone whose life looks good from a distance may feel awful inside. Likewise, someone who is experiencing hard times may nevertheless have a sense of wellbeing. Wellbeing can be described in many ways – feeling that your life is fine, feeling happy, feeling content. A lack of wellbeing is when a person feels unhappy, insecure, worried, depressed or angry.

Just like you, your child experiences wellbeing (or a lack thereof), but it is generally harder for her to have a clear awareness of her level of wellbeing and to communicate it to others. Your child's experience is limited by the number of years she has been alive. If your child feels unhappy and has been unhappy since she was a toddler, she may not know what it would be like to feel happy. It can be hard for children to make a judgement about whether their level of wellbeing is what it should be. Children who lack a sense of wellbeing may feel anxious, angry or irritable. They may find it hard to enjoy activities, be preoccupied with their negative mood, find it hard to cooperate with people or be uninterested in learning. Your child's level of wellbeing also influences her family and social relationships.

For your child to experience wellbeing, her emotional needs must be met adequately by the people around her. The parent–child relationship is the place where your child's emotional needs are usually met, and there is a huge amount that you can do to meet those needs.

Elise, ten years old, is a happy and confident girl. She enjoys school, has friends and gets along with her family. She is enjoying life because she feels secure in her relationships with her parents, knows from experience they will help her when she needs them, and is confident about her ability to do the things that are expected of her at school and home.

Emotional intelligence

Emotional intelligence is knowledge and skills related to emotions. Some would argue that emotional intelligence is as important as the traditional notion of intelligence (reasoning and thinking abilities). People who understand their own feelings and who can make judgements about other people's feelings are better equipped to deal with the challenges of life. In addition to having awareness of their feelings, people also need to know how to manage them so that they don't get in the way of their goals. For example, when angry, a person may be tempted to speak rudely. Yet if the person requires someone's help, they would disadvantage themselves by being rude (it would reduce the other person's motivation to help). A person with high emotional intelligence would recognise that they are tempted to be rude because they feel angry, and would either be able to mask their feelings, or calm themselves so that they are able to speak pleasantly to the person whose help they need.

Children gradually learn about their feelings and how to cope with them. Emotions can influence emotional intelligence in a number of ways. For example, if your child is often upset, she will be less likely to develop an awareness of others' feelings (being so often overwhelmed with her own feelings). Having intense bouts of distress can also interfere with development of emotional intelligence because it is much easier to control emotions when they are less intense. A child who experiences intense emotions (especially negative emotions such as anger) is less able to practise managing her feelings.

Trent is a four-year-old boy who has a secure attachment relationship with his parents. They speak to Trent about his feelings and other people's feelings and soothe him when he is distressed. Such supportive parenting has allowed him to gain awareness of what he is feeling and what other people are feeling. This means that his ability to regulate his emotions is as developed as it should be for a four-year-old and he is able to concentrate and get along with people, and recover from upsets.

Behaviour

It is important for your child's adjustment (and your sanity) that she is cooperative and behaves in a socially acceptable manner. Emotions are closely linked with behaviour. Difficult behaviour – disobedience, rudeness, and lack of cooperation – often stems from emotional turmoil. A child who is angry, sad, or feels that people don't like her will find it difficult to behave herself. It makes sense: if we feel criticised or undervalued, our motivation to cooperate is reduced. A lot of children's distress comes out in their behaviour. Children have a limited ability to stand back from a situation and to put feelings into words and this makes children susceptible to 'acting out' their feelings.

Billy is a nine-year-old boy who often feels angry and irritable. He gets easily annoyed with other children and with his family. He yells and often doesn't do as his teacher and his parents ask him. He feels they are just trying to boss him around. Because of his irritable mood, he overreacts to minor events in his day (not finding a pair of socks, a child taking his pencil in class). If things don't go his way, he becomes overwhelmed with anger. On the surface, he is badly behaved. Underneath, he has emotional problems.

Self-esteem

Emotions can impact on a child's self-esteem. For example, a child with emotional problems will see that her peers cope better with school than she does. This comparison may affect a child's self-esteem – she may feel she is not as competent as other children the same age.

Cassandra, eleven years old, feels insecure and worried a lot of the time. She can see that her classmates can cope with situations that she tries to avoid. Going on school camps feels unbearable, as does speaking in front of the class. Often she gets the feeling people don't like her. Compared with her peers, she experiences much more stress when in new situations, because of her low self-esteem and lack of faith in her ability to cope.

Social competence

Children who have emotional problems can run into social problems in two ways. Anxious and depressed children often withdraw into themselves, show a lack of confidence and so may become vulnerable to bullying. Other children might find them unappealing because they look glum and

11

downhearted. Angry children tend to lash out at their peers, and so can quickly become unpopular and ostracised. In contrast, children who experience positive emotions are likely to be helpful, to play well with others, and to be socially skilled (not losing their temper, being able to wait their turn).

> *Derek, eight, has moved school for the third time in as many years. But it only took a week for him to put most of the class offside. When someone is in his way, he pushes them; he doesn't cooperate and insists other children listen to his ideas about what games to play. The other children find it is not worth the trouble to hang around Derek – he disrupts their games, and does and says things that hurt other children. It's easy for teachers and parents to focus on Derek's appalling behaviour, but emotionally he is unhappy and tense, and so normal and pleasant social interactions become nearly impossible for him.*

School performance

Your child's performance in the classroom is influenced by her emotions. Anxiety and anger can easily disrupt your child's attention or motivation, and she may fail to perform at the level at which she is capable. Not all academic problems relate to emotional problems, but research does show that emotional problems (for example, even mild anxiety) interfere with children's learning and academic achievement. Negative emotions can preoccupy your child and reduce her attention and energy for schoolwork. This is true for adults as well as children – if we're worried or angry, it can be hard to concentrate on our work. Emotional health doesn't automatically lead to good school learning, but it gives your child an advantage. All things being equal, she is more likely to reach her potential if she is emotionally healthy.

Han is a seven-year-old girl with anxiety. She worries whether her work is good enough, spends a lot of time wondering if her classmates like her and worries her mum won't return to pick her up from school. While the teacher is explaining how to add numbers and count by 10s, she is wondering if her mum is okay, and if she will have someone to play with at lunchtime. She is distracted by her worries and isn't giving full attention to her work. Motivation also lags. How can Han get excited about counting by 10s if she is preoccupied with all the things that might go wrong?

SOME POSSIBLE PATHWAYS FROM FEELINGS TO OUTCOMES

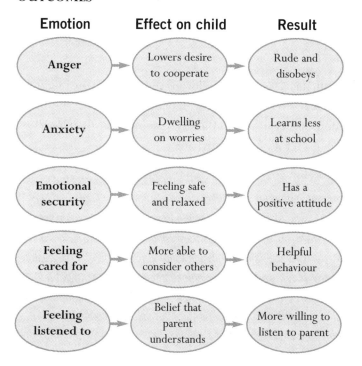

Emotion	Effect on child	Result
Anger	Lowers desire to cooperate	Rude and disobeys
Anxiety	Dwelling on worries	Learns less at school
Emotional security	Feeling safe and relaxed	Has a positive attitude
Feeling cared for	More able to consider others	Helpful behaviour
Feeling listened to	Belief that parent understands	More willing to listen to parent

There are a few things to note about the flowchart. First of all, it does not deal with 'objective reality' (if there is such a thing), but rather with what is happening from the child's point of view. Children and adults are not so much influenced by 'objective reality' but rather how they perceive things to be. There can be a big difference between what parents think is happening, and what the child actually experiences. For example, a parent may think that they treat their child fairly and listen to their point of view – the child's experiences of the conversations they have might be totally different. It is the child's perception that will be most influential on how the child feels and behaves – not the parent's version.

The second point to note is that feelings may exert their influence in a number of ways: by affecting the child's level of motivation, attitude and behaviour.

HOW DO CHILDREN'S EMOTIONS AFFECT THEIR PARENTS?

After all this talk about children's emotions, you might be wondering, 'What about my feelings?'. Indeed, children's emotions affect not only themselves, but also their parents. Let's consider a typical scenario:

Jane, a 35-year-old mother, works part-time and spends the rest of her time caring for her two children, ten-month-old Tom and Lucy, three years. She is glad to be able to spend a few days a week with them, but she also finds it demanding. Many days, Tom is grizzly. Now she is driving home with him screaming in the back seat. When they get home, Jane somehow manages to get him to sleep. But the challenges don't end there: Lucy is going through a 'phase' and throws herself on the floor crying because the television is switched off for dinner. Jane knows that tantrums are often a part of growing up, but coping with them can be demanding and exhausting. Jane is not really sure how she should be responding to them. Is Lucy trying to control her with her performances? If she comforts Lucy, is she encouraging bad behaviour?

If Jane comforts Lucy, rather than encouraging bad behaviour, Jane is showing that she cares about Lucy's feelings and that she can help her to calm down. Lucy's tantrums are part of her emotional development, and are not designed to 'control' her mother. Her tantrums are a sign that Lucy feels overwhelmed by her negative feelings. Jane needs to set limits though – if every time Lucy cried, she let her watch TV, it would not be helping Lucy to follow the routine that is needed for the family (which includes having a quiet time to enjoy dinner together). Lucy is young and it is hard for her to deal with the disappointment of not being able to watch TV when she wants to. Jane can help her by being calm (speaking calmly), being clear and consistent (always having the TV off during dinner), and showing Lucy she cares about her feelings (e.g. 'I know you want to watch TV now, but we need to have dinner. You'll get to watch it again tomorrow when "Thomas the Tank Engine" is on. How about you help me to get the table ready for dinner?' or some other task that might interest Lucy and help to engage her.). If Lucy continues to cry and tantrum, Jane might say 'It's okay, do you want a hug?' If Lucy is thrashing wildly on the floor Jane might need to stand clear and return every few minutes and watch for signs that Lucy is able to accept soothing from her.

Jane's experiences echo countless other parents' daily lives with young children. Looking at the demands on Jane, it can be seen that her children's emotions are central to what is going on. Her children's emotions show through their behaviour – Tom cries; Lucy has tantrums.

Mood contagion – catching someone else's feelings

This goes both ways – your child can influence your mood, and you can influence your child's mood. Parents often say that the chances of their children misbehaving increases when they are having a bad day themselves. This could be because the children are sensing the parent's tension, and then feel unsettled themselves – which is then shown in their behaviour. Parents may not be aware of behaving any differently, and may be surprised to learn that their child knows how they are feeling, but emotion is communicated in many ways: tone of voice (even slight differences in intonation can say a lot about how we're feeling – frustrated, down, enthusiastic); facial expressions (most of the time our facial expressions are not under our conscious control); subtle (and not so subtle) differences in how parents respond to the child. One reason that children are affected by parental moods is because of their dependence on their parents.

Thinking about children's feelings takes time and effort

Getting it right often takes extra effort. An analogy can be drawn with nutrition – the easy option may be to have take-away every night, but it is more healthy and time-consuming to plan and prepare nutritious meals. It is a bit like that with emotions – to just react any old how is easy, but to consider what your child needs, to be thoughtful about your response, takes time and effort. Parenting in a way that is considerate of the child's feelings can be emotionally exhausting. Being with a child who requires a lot of soothing and interaction can leave you feeling drained.

PARENTS' EMOTIONAL NEEDS

Everyone has emotional needs, regardless of their age. Hopefully as people get older they become better at recognising their feelings and having a range of strategies for dealing with them – having a chat to someone, changing how they think, and countless other strategies that can be used to change or manage feelings. While this book focuses on how parents (and others) can meet children's emotional needs, this is in no way to downplay the fact that you have emotional needs as well.

While parents ideally meet their children's emotional needs, the reverse is not the case (children should not have to meet their parents' emotional needs). In some instances, parents look to their children to give them support and meet their emotional needs. In such cases the child may be said to be 'parentified' or 'adultified' – that is, taking on some of the worries and responsibilities that belong to adults, not children. The parent–child roles are sometimes reversed. For example, if the parent is going through a hard time emotionally, the child may take on the role of caring for the parent.

Maria is a 38-year-old mother married to George. They have three children: Nick nine years, Dimitri six years, and Sophie two years. Maria suffers from depression from time to time and tends to be anxious. She is often worried about the state of the family business, the family's finances, and Sophie's health problems. George works long hours and even when he is home, he tends to be preoccupied with his own worries, so it's hard for Maria to use him as an emotional support. Nick is a perceptive nine-year-old and when he sees that his mother is worried or down, he asks her what's wrong. Maria tells him about her worries. Because Nick is such a good listener, Maria momentarily forgets that he is only nine years old, and instead talks to him the way she would to an adult. She tells him of the financial troubles, Sophie's health problems, and about her feelings of depression. Nick doesn't have the emotional maturity to support his mother, but he wants to help, so he is quiet and listens. But inside it affects him. He becomes worried and angry because he is burdened by adult worries that he as a child can't carry. Maria doesn't really know what is going on. She cares for her children deeply and would be quite taken aback if she realised the extent to which she is emotionally depending on her son. In addition to having adult worries, the conversations affect Nick another way: he is not able to access his mother for support. When he has a bad day at school, or has worries of his own, he finds it hard to talk to his mother about them, because he knows she's not feeling well as it is, and he instinctively doesn't want to add to her problems.

TUNING IN TO YOUR CHILD'S EMOTIONS

From her first day of life, your child experiences emotions. These emotions influence her in many ways. They affect her behaviour, how she sees the world, how she reacts to other people, and they determine (to a large extent) her level of wellbeing. Considering the powerful links between your child's emotions and her development and ability to get the most out of life, it might seem surprising that children's emotions aren't given more attention. Parents are exposed to a lot of information about children's nutritional needs, children's behaviour (including behaviour management strategies) and issues like school readiness. Of course these are very important issues in a child's life and clearly deserve attention. However, emotions are just as important.

Here are some possible reasons why children's emotions tend to be neglected in discussions and parent education programs:

Emotions can be relatively invisible

It can be easier to tell if a child has problems with her motor and language development (e.g. not walking or talking when she should be) than with her emotions. Behaviour is also highly visible. If a child has severe tantrums it can be seen a mile off. Emotions can be harder to pin down.

It may not be obvious that a child is emotionally troubled. Sure, there will be some sign – maybe she will be withdrawn or uncooperative. But those behaviours can be interpreted in many different ways. Any number of explanations could be given for the child's behaviour that have nothing to do with her emotions. A child with severe temper tantrums might be seen as strong-willed, rather than having problems regulating her emotions; a child who is withdrawn may be seen as having a quiet nature, rather than feeling sad. Symptoms of emotional problems can be interpreted in many ways. Often a non-emotional explanation will seem more likely than an emotional one. This can be a self-perpetuating cycle – because a child's emotions are not talked about much, parents may assume that emotional problems are rare. In contrast, parents often hear about behavioural issues, and so more quickly consider their child's issues in terms of behaviour.

It can be tempting to dismiss your child's emotions

Children require a lot of emotional care – and they frequently display their emotions. This can place a burden on caregivers because a lot of patience and effort is required to meet children's emotional needs. There can be a tendency to dismiss a child's emotions as unimportant or trivial, rather than as real experiences that she feels as deeply as adults would. Many adults would pay more attention to another adult crying inconsolably than a child crying the same way. While it is more common to see a crying child than a crying adult, this does not mean that a child's experiences are any less genuine, or deserve less attention.

Handling sudden changes in children's emotions

Children can show sudden changes in their emotions – and this can encourage adults to dismiss children's emotions. One minute your toddler is laughing and the next she is crying. It can be easy to dismiss such feelings as superficial. Because your child is less emotionally mature than you, she is less adept at regulating her emotions. This is one reason for the sudden shifts in emotions that can be seen, especially in younger children.

Addressing emotions is exhausting

If you take your child's feelings seriously, then there is an imperative to act. If your child really experiences distress then it follows logically that you need to think about how to respond to it. If you are feeling stretched just providing daily physical care, this may feel too much, and so in defence you may block out thoughts of your child's feelings so that you don't feel overwhelmed.

It's easy to focus on your child's behaviour

Behaviour is not the whole story. Your child may be well behaved, but emotionally unwell. Children may behave well out of fear and anxiety. Children who have behavioural problems also have emotional problems. They have trouble managing their feelings; they may feel that things aren't fair for them. It can be easier to define a behaviour problem, and to focus on it. For you to understand your child, and to respond to her in a way that is helpful for her development, you need to think about both her behaviour and her feelings. Behaviour cannot really be understood without understanding your child's feelings.

Summary

▶ Every aspect of your child's life can be affected by her emotional health.

(▶) Emotional problems may disrupt your child's learning, behaviour, self-esteem, social skills and wellbeing.

▶ Meeting your child's emotional needs is an important part of parenting.

(▶) Meeting your child's emotional needs is a way for you to give her the best chance of having a positive self-esteem, ability to cope with life's challenges and the ability to reach her potential, socially and in other spheres.

What are children's emotional needs?

Children are born with emotional needs in much the same way that they are born with needs for nutrition and physical care. Just as children who receive the nutrients they need are likely to grow up physically strong and healthy, and children who don't are likely to fall ill, so it is with emotional needs. Children whose emotional needs are met have a much better chance of growing up psychologically healthy.

If your child's emotional needs are met he is likely to have:

★ a healthy self-esteem. By meeting your child's emotional needs you are sending him a powerful and clear message that he is loved and cared for. Therefore, he has evidence that he is worthwhile. Self-esteem is built on actual experiences. Emotional nurturing ensures a solid foundation on which to build self-worth.

★ positive, trusting relationships with other people

★ the ability to regulate his emotions

★ a happier disposition than a child whose needs are not met.

In contrast, if your child's emotional needs are not met he is likely to experience:

★ low self-esteem. Your child may have a lingering feeling that he is not as good as other people. This can affect his confidence, how he interacts with other people, and how happy he is.

★ lack of trust in other people. Your child may be wary of other people and find it hard to believe that other people care about him, or that they can be trusted.

★ poor emotional regulation. Your child may have trouble regulating his feelings, and this can land him in trouble socially, academically and may prevent him from reaching his potential.

★ lack of wellbeing. Because emotional needs are basic human needs, if your child does not have his needs met he is more likely to be unhappy.

Key emotional needs

There are seven key emotional needs that all children have regardless of their age or cultural background:

1　to have a secure relationship with a parent or other caregiver

2　to receive help with managing their emotions

3　to receive emotional support, particularly when they are experiencing difficulties

4　to have a sense of belonging

5　to feel loved

6　to feel accepted and approved of

7　to have clear expectations, routines and boundaries.

Let's look at each one in turn.

THE NEED FOR A SECURE RELATIONSHIP

Children around the world have an inborn need for a relationship with their parents or caregivers. An attachment relationship is a lasting emotional bond. As long as there is regular contact with parents, children become attached to them. Children also form attachment relationships with other important people in their life, such as grandparents and siblings. Usually children have one or two primary attachments, most commonly with their parents.

A child's attachment to a parent is believed to serve a biological survival function because it means that the child tries to stay close to his attachment figure. Staying close to his parents increases a child's chances of survival because he is less likely to be hurt or lost.

The difference between children is not so much whether they form an attachment relationship (because the vast majority do), but the security of that relationship. The security of your child's attachment influences his emotional development, social skills, ability to manage his emotions and self-esteem.

A gift

Helping your child to establish a secure relationship with you is a gift. It is a gift that helps to set him up for life: it increases his chances of having emotional health and healthy relationships in the future.

Here are some examples of the everyday behaviour of children who have a secure attachment:

Eight-year-old Lizzy has cut her finger and she comes to her dad, clutching her finger and crying.

Lizzy has a secure attachment to her father, so when she feels hurt, she goes to him for comfort and reassurance.

Hue has made the local basketball team. She is so excited that she calls her mum at work to tell her the exciting news.

Hue has a secure attachment with her mother. This means that she is comfortable with sharing her emotional experiences with her and wants to share her excitement.

A parent means security

When a child develops an attachment with a parent, the parent represents a secure base. The parent is seen as a refuge from danger, a person who provides warmth, nurture and protection. In insecure attachment, the child is in a bind – on the one hand the parent represents his secure base, on the other hand he cannot trust that the parent will be there for him. This can lead to anxiety, anger and clinginess. In insecure attachment, the child is still 'attached', but feels unable to depend on his parent. It is important for your child's emotional health that he feels confident he can depend on his attachment figure. Children who don't have this security are vulnerable to emotional problems.

Clinginess and confidence

Depending on you as a secure base means that when your child is scared, upset or feeling unwell, he wants to be close to you. You may have noticed that in new surroundings, or when your child is running a fever, he is more clingy and may not want to let you out of sight. This is an example of attachment behaviour increasing because of the stress and uncertainty your child feels. When your child is feeling unsure or stressed, he will come to you because you are his source of security. Verbal reassurance may be enough, but if he is feeling particularly distressed, he may need physical contact to regain his sense of wellbeing.

When your child feels fine, he will alternate between exploring his environment and returning to you when he is tired, hungry or scared. For example, your toddler might move away from you to play with toys, and then when tired or wanting reassurance, he returns to you. A securely attached child knows from experience that you will be there for him when he needs you. This makes him feel at ease. Securely attached children are confident enough to explore their environment because they don't have to be constantly on the look out worrying about the location of their parent. Insecurely attached children are not confident that anyone will be there for them if anything goes wrong, and so tend to be restricted in their exploration.

Harry, a two-year-old, is at playgroup with his mother Peta. For the past six weeks they have attended this playgroup and each visit Harry spends more time away from Peta. She sits to have coffee and chat with other mums while Harry explores the sandpit and toys. When he trips over, or gets lonely or uncomfortable, he waddles back to Peta. She talks soothingly, gives him a hug if he wants one, and off he goes again. Harry is using his mother as a secure base – somewhere he can return to when the world gets challenging. When children are scared or uncomfortable they seek comfort from their attachment figures. In essence, the relationship gives them renewed emotional strength, a feeling they are not alone, and this allows them to venture out again.

While all children develop an attachment to their parents (provided that they live with them or see them on a regular basis), the security of that attachment varies. Security of attachment can range on a continuum from secure to insecure. It is possible for a child to have a secure attachment with one parent and an insecure attachment with another parent. This is because attachment is about the relationship a child has with another person; it is not a characteristic of the child.

Obstacles to quality care

The quality of care you give your child is the main determinant of his security of attachment to you.

It may be hard for you to provide consistent and high quality care if:

★ you have mental health problems such as anxiety and depression

★ you received poor-quality parenting

★ your child has characteristics that make him more difficult to care for (e.g. a child who is very demanding, or not responsive because of prematurity)

★ poverty and other life stresses compromise the energy you have left for caring for your child

★ there is substantial, consistent conflict between you and your partner.

The best time to start is now

A child who does not have his emotional needs met at one point in time is by no means doomed. Beginning to meet your child's needs at any time is a positive step that can help him enormously. A child who is used to not having his needs met may be slow to respond. Yet even adults who did not have their needs met as children can alter their emotional development. These changes take time, but there is reason to be hopeful about people's capacity to recover from adverse circumstances.

THE NEED FOR HELP WITH MANAGING EMOTIONS

Children of all ages require help with managing their emotions. Helping your child with his emotions involves:

★ taking his feelings seriously

★ intervening as early as possible if your child is upset (the longer he is upset, the harder it will be to calm him down)

★ helping him to calm down if he is angry or upset

★ using soothing strategies such as talking calmly (e.g. 'I know you don't want to have a bath, but you need to now. It won't be that bad, you can have your hot chocolate afterwards.') and physical contact (e.g. carrying a baby, hugging, a reassuring pat on the shoulder).

Some of the benefits of helping your child with emotional regulation are that it:

★ helps your child to learn how to manage his emotions

★ helps your child to be in a calm state more often

★ shows your child that his feelings matter

★ shows your child that his parents care about him

★ helps parents to feel closer to their child

★ helps you to establish a relationship with your child where you are able to help him when he needs it.

Janice, mother of ten-year-old William, used to leave him alone when he was angry or upset. He often acted like he didn't want her around him at those times. He would storm off and go to his room and cry, or throw things around. When he emerged from his room, he was calmer, but still irritable. William had problems regulating his emotions and was more frequently upset than would be expected for someone his age. This interfered with his relationship with his teacher, with his friendships, and was disruptive for his family. Janice tried a different approach. Instead of letting William sort himself out, she tried to be supportive. When it looked like he was getting upset, instead of demanding he behave, she asked him what was wrong. To her surprise, he would tell her (someone was annoying him, or he had a bad day at school). Then she would say 'that's no good' to show him she cared about his feelings, and then tried to solve the problem with him. Sometimes just having his mother listen made William feel calmer, and he could interact with people more easily. Of course, there were times he held back, but his mother just persisted and let him know that she wanted to know what he was feeling and wanted to help him. After a few months, William was able to open up to her about some deeper issues. It took a few months for him to work up the courage to disclose to his mother that he was being bullied at school. Once he did, she was able to contact the school and design a plan of action with them to address the issue. Janice knows that the work she has done to listen to William consistently has paid off in many ways. He now goes to her much sooner when he is upset (instead of acting up and annoying everyone else in the family), and she feels closer to him.

THE NEED FOR EMOTIONAL SUPPORT

We all need support, children especially. Being supportive means showing your child that he is not alone with his experiences or problems. These are the steps involved in providing support:

★ listening to your child's feelings and experiences

★ taking your child's perspective seriously

★ expressing concern for your child's wellbeing (e.g. saying 'I'm sorry to hear you're having a hard time with your friend', giving a sympathetic look, or showing affection).

★ engaging in a conversation about problem-solving – helping your child to consider how he might handle the situation, what you might do to help him, how he might make himself feel better.

Support is about letting your child know that he is not alone with his problems, but rather that you are there to help him. Your child needs to be able to speak about his emotions and experiences, both positive and negative. If your child knows from experience that he will be listened to, he is more likely to talk to you openly.

THE NEED FOR A SENSE OF BELONGING

The desire to belong is present in children and adults. For children, it is important that they feel they belong to their family. This might seem a foregone conclusion – they are part of the family, and surely they realise it. Sometimes, it is more complicated than simply being born into a family. Children can feel alienated in their own family, and may not feel they really belong. Two things need to happen for us to feel we belong:

1   a sense of welcome. Is the family welcoming of this child?

2   to feel valuable to the group. In a family the value might be related to the child knowing he is loved, fun to be with, helpful, and so on.

Day-to-day interactions have a big impact on whether your child feels he belongs. How is he spoken to? What roles does he have? Is there time for fun and games when the family interacts in a relaxed manner? You may need to go out of your way to help your child feel he belongs. Your child is dependent on his home's 'emotional climate' for nurture and a sense of belonging. It is painful for a child to feel he doesn't belong in the family.

THE NEED TO FEEL LOVED

Many parents may think, 'Of course my child knows he is loved' (regardless of what is going on), but your child's beliefs about what others think and feel about him are dependent on what actually happens in daily life. If your child is criticised often, or spoken to harshly, or there is frequent conflict between you and your child, he may feel unloved.

You might say 'You know I love you', but your interactions may not bear that out. <u>Feeling loved</u> is a great emotional boost – it helps your child to feel secure. If he feels you don't love him, chances are he won't love himself. The fallout from that might be difficulty interacting with people, a sense of insecurity and low self-esteem. To ensure that your child feels loved, it is important to act in a loving way towards him: speaking respectfully, smiling, showing affection, saying positive things to him, and so on.

THE NEED FOR ACCEPTANCE AND APPROVAL

There are times when you need to make it clear to your child that his behaviour is unacceptable or that his action is not approved of (e.g. hitting a sibling, swearing). Yet overall, your child should have the feeling that he is accepted and approved of, otherwise he is likely to feel bad about himself. Lack of approval is also likely to make your child feel anxious. If your child thinks that he is a bad person, then his behaviour is likely to reflect that. A child who believes he is a good person is more likely to internalise the standards of behaviour that his parents and teachers try to instil in him. Sometimes children behave in a way that makes it hard for parents to approve of them – all that the parents see is the negative behaviour. At such times, it is important to consciously seek out positive aspects of the child to comment on and praise (helping to clean up, being polite, carrying the groceries).

THE NEED TO HAVE CLEAR EXPECTATIONS, ROUTINES AND BOUNDARIES

Your child needs to know that you have clear expectations of his behaviour, to have a reasonable amount of routine in his daily life, and to be given appropriate boundaries (in terms of privacy and psychological space).

Children who are not given boundaries and clear expectations live in a chaotic world. This feels uncomfortable for them (chaos feels uncomfortable for most adults too). Children have less ability than adults to set routines and order. Parents who provide routines help their children to experience the world as an orderly and reasonably predictable place. Expectations, routines and boundaries will help your child develop a sense of security and to function well in family, school and peer settings.

ATTACHMENT AND EMOTIONAL DEVELOPMENT

There is some evidence that children's attachment security is linked to their emotional development. Children with secure attachment have shown more positive emotional development than insecurely attached children. Anger, fear and joy have been investigated in children aged nine months to three years.

Children were found to experience more anger as they entered the toddler years, regardless of security of attachment. However, securely attached children then had a decline in anger as they reached three years of age. Insecurely attached children continued to experience higher levels of anger as they grew to three years of age. Likewise, fear increased over time in children who were insecurely attached. In contrast, securely attached children became less fearful over time. Insecurely attached children showed less joy as they aged, compared to securely attached children. So the security of attachment has ramifications for children's emotional development and wellbeing.

Four types of attachment have been identified. These can be divided into two groups: secure and insecure. The three insecure types can be further divided into avoidant, anxious (also called ambivalent/resistant) and disoriented/disorganised.

Secure attachment

Beatrice is a four-year-old who has a secure attachment to both parents. Beatrice and her parents enjoy their time together. There is a relaxed feeling about their relationship. They show affection and, most of the time, they are happy with each other. When Beatrice is upset, for example when she was sad that her pet goldfish died, her parents talked to her and knew how to soothe her. They listened to her, gave her hugs and helped her to come to terms with her loss. Of course, there are times when Beatrice misbehaves, but her parents make it clear to her what they expect and they are able to correct the undesirable behaviour and move on without negative feelings lingering.

This is the ideal attachment style. About 70 percent of children in community samples are securely attached. In this type of relationship both parent and child are at ease with each other. The securely attached child knows from experience that his parent will meet his emotional and physical needs. The parent responds promptly and empathically to their child's distress. A secure attachment relationship is often satisfying for both parent and child. The securely attached child feels his needs are met and the parent is likely to feel close to their child and to feel competent in their parenting role (though this is not always the case).

Emotions, both positive and negative, are acknowledged and dealt with openly and kindly in a secure attachment relationship. The child seeks comfort and support when distressed and uncertain, and the parent responds promptly to his needs.

Using you as a secure base

A securely attached child is able to use his parent as a secure base. This child alternates between exploring his environment and returning to his parent for comfort and a feeling of security. The child seeks his parent when he is lonely, wants company, or is feeling tired or distressed. When young, a child may seek comfort by wanting to be close to the parent or clambering onto the parent's lap. Older children can be more easily comforted and reassured by words. The principle is still the same – children seek their parents' support when they need it, because their experience has taught them that their parents will be there for them.

Even adolescents and adults who are securely attached seek contact with their attachment figures when upset or emotionally in need. The contact may be in person, by phone or email, but the idea is the same – a desire to have contact with attachment figure(s) when he is experiencing joys or sorrows, and a desire to share daily experiences.

Positive effects on your child

Secure attachment promotes resilience in children. Children who are securely attached have a number of advantages over insecurely attached children. These are:

★ a higher level of emotional health

★ more positive social relationships (they are less likely to be victims of bullying, more likely to trust their friends and to be able to have intimacy in relationships in adolescence and adulthood)

★ a better coping ability

★ a better ability to manage their feelings.

Securely attached children see themselves as lovable and worthy of being looked after. They view other people as generally trustworthy and worth knowing. Their perception of the world is that it is a reasonably predictable place where they can be competent and have their needs met. These positive beliefs affect how children approach other people, new experiences and the world.

Parental behaviour that may encourage secure attachment

Parental care influences the likelihood of a child becoming securely attached. Research around the world has shown the types of parenting that lead to secure and insecure attachment.

Be responsive

Responding quickly and consistently to your child's distress increases the likelihood that he will become securely attached to you. Responsive parenting means that you respond when your child wants comfort, that is, when he is crying, grizzling or showing other signs of distress. Rather than waiting till your child is crying loudly, respond when he is showing the first signs of distress or discomfort.

Responsiveness includes responding to your child's efforts to interact with you, for example when he speaks or makes eye contact.

Comfort when it's needed

One study found that securely and insecurely attached children were physically held just as much by their mothers. The difference was in the timing of contact, not the amount. Mothers of securely attached children held and cuddled them when they were upset (as well as when they were happy and neutral), while insecurely attached children were only held when they were happy or neutral in their feelings. When insecurely attached children became upset and/or sought comfort, their parents rebuffed, criticised or ignored them.

Respond with reassurance

By responding to your child's negative emotions in a reassuring way, you are communicating to your child that:

★ it is okay to feel sad and angry (everyone does at some time)

★ his feelings matter

★ together you can cope with these emotions

★ he will get support when he needs it (not just when he is smiling).

Try to be sensitive

Secure attachment is related to parental sensitivity towards a child. Does your child need cuddles? Would he rather be left to play? Is he feeling tired and needs unwinding? Looking carefully at what your child is trying to communicate (verbally or by his behaviour) helps you to have sensitive interactions.

Show warmth

Children thrive on a cheerful, soothing tone of voice, a loving gaze, affection and smiles. Here are some ways to demonstrate warmth:

★ speak in a warm tone of voice

★ smile at your child

★ give him a hug

★ have an affectionate pet name for your child (e.g. 'how is my bumblebee today?')

★ praise your child.

Meaningful connection

If your child smiles and you smile in return, you've made a meaningful connection. This is sometimes called 'synchrony'. Lack of synchrony would be if your child is trying to engage your attention and you are stony-faced. Research into children's emotional development has shown that synchrony is important for a child's mood and expression of emotion. Infants are affected by their parents' expressions of emotion in face-to-face interactions. In one study, the sequence of interactions between a parent and child was examined in detail. It was found that infants had a much higher chance of showing happiness if their mother expressed happiness towards them. If the mother wasn't positive, the infant only had a minimal likelihood of showing happiness. Infants who have distressed or depressed parents are more likely to show distress themselves – they might look blank, uninterested in their environment, and cry more easily compared to children whose parents are not depressed.

Patterns of emotional expression in secure attachment

When children are securely attached, they are comfortable in displaying (and when older, discussing) their feelings. For the parents' part, they respond by accepting their child's feelings and providing support and reassurance. They do not make their child feel ashamed about his emotions.

Relationship between secure attachment and independence

Children who are securely attached are most likely to be appropriately independent as they grow up. They feel secure knowing that there are people on whom they can rely. Insecurely attached children, on the other hand, are not sure there is anyone they can rely on. This makes it harder for them to be independent – if they were to get into trouble, who would help them?

Secure attachment in adulthood

Securely attached adults tend to have relationships that are satisfying. They feel comfortable relying on others when they need help and feel competent in dealing with life's challenges. They are not overly dependent, but do recognise the importance of other people and the support they bring to their life. They are aware of their feelings and generally manage them well. They are less likely to feel distressed than insecurely attached adults, and they are able to disclose their feelings.

Avoidant attachment

Larry is a five-year-old boy with an avoidant attachment to his parents. During his life, his parents have been stressed and unable to respond to him when he was upset. They had trouble coping with their own problems and they were determined that Larry needed to learn to not be demanding. When Larry used to cry as a baby, they would leave him alone. If he was happy, they would play with him and respond enthusiastically. They wanted to make sure they didn't reward whingeing. Larry has learnt to suppress his feelings. If he starts to get worried or sad, he tends to keep it to himself. The main sign that something is wrong may be that he goes quiet and there is a blank expression on his face. This is not something he does consciously, it just happens; this is the way he has learnt to manage his emotions. Larry manages at school, but has a tendency to worry and finds it hard to mix with other children. He is not confident about approaching his teacher – he doesn't really trust her. Larry's parents are proud of him; he is overall a well-behaved child and developing normally in many ways. However, they do feel somewhat emotionally distant from him. They wish he would open up more so they could talk to him. When they ask what is wrong, he says 'nothing'. They wonder whether it will be hard for him to communicate his feelings as he gets older.

The avoidant attachment relationship is characterised by aloofness between the child and parent (about 20 percent of children fall into this category). Superficially, the relationship may seem fine, but both parent and child feel a lack of emotional closeness. The relationship has a 'formal' quality, a certain emotional distance. Emotions tend not to be discussed or addressed, especially negative emotions (anger, sadness, frustration or loneliness).

Using you as a secure base

When a child has an insecure attachment to his parent, he is unable to use his parent as a secure base. Through experience, the child has learnt that his parents will not respond supportively to his negative emotions. Over repeated experiences of not having his emotional needs met, he has learnt to try to keep negative emotions to himself.

On the surface, this child may appear fine. A good example of this is in the 'Strange Situation', a method of assessing the security of a child's attachment to a parent or caregiver. This procedure involves carefully observing how the child behaves when brought into a new setting with his parent. First, the child's behaviour is observed while his parent is present. Then observations are made of the child's reaction to the parent leaving the room (only a stranger remains with the child), the child's behaviour while the parent is gone, and also his behaviour when the parent returns. In the 'Strange Situation', children who are avoidantly attached tend to look unconcerned and aloof. They don't explore as much as the securely attached child because they are not sure if the attachment figure will be there for them. They try not to show negative feelings. For example, when the parent leaves the room, they may show no reaction to being left with a stranger in a strange place. Some researchers argue that this type of behaviour shouldn't be interpreted as insecure attachment, but rather that the child is mature and self-sufficient. However, there is evidence that this is not the case.

★ Physiological measures, including heart rate, indicate that at the time of separation, the child is feeling stressed, but is not showing it.

★ Avoidantly attached children (and indeed adults) have less
satisfactory relationships, are more likely to feel uncomfortable
with intimacy, want to be excessively self-reliant, and are more
likely to have emotional and behavioural problems.

This child has difficulty using his parent as a secure base
because he is not convinced that the parent will provide
comfort when he needs it. He nevertheless wants to receive
comfort and he seems as though he is trying to suppress his
need to cling to his parent. Another indication of insecurity
is that he tends to keep his attachment figure in sight and is
not able to freely engage with the environment. It has been
argued that these children are too preoccupied about the
parent's whereabouts to be interested in exploring the
environment, and that they do not venture away because they
are concerned that the parent will vanish. (Of course, some
level of monitoring of the parent's whereabouts is normal.)

Implications for your relationship with your child

Because the avoidant attachment style involves not discussing
emotions and emotional distance, you may feel rebuffed by
your child. You may wish that your child would come to you
for comfort and speak to you about their feelings. You may
wonder why your child is so aloof. Avoidant attachment can
make parenting more difficult than if your child were
securely attached because:

★ your child is reluctant to discuss his feelings. This makes it
hard for you to figure out what is happening. Your child may
seem upset or downcast, but when asked what is wrong, he
doesn't specify. Even when things occur that you know have
upset your child, when you try to discuss the matter, your

child may refuse to talk about it. It is no wonder you may feel shut out and powerless to help him.

★ your child may find it hard to be soothed, so your efforts at calming your child may not work. You might understandably become frustrated and may disengage (that is, stop trying to comfort him). Your child may insist on being left alone. If this is a continual pattern of responding to distress it can be problematic because he is not open to support and comfort. You may often feel you don't have many options in such a case: if you do as your child says and leave him alone, you are not trying to soothe him when he is most upset, and if you continue to try to soothe your child, it can exacerbate his distress.

Effects on your child

Children who are insecurely attached have a lower level of wellbeing than securely attached children. Often negative emotions are hidden and fester under the surface only to emerge in peer interactions. When upset, these children don't feel comfortable about receiving support and are likely to try to deal with problems by themselves. There is a sense of shame about needing to depend on others. They may find it hard to deal with stressful situations, and are at higher risk for anxiety, depression and behaviour problems.

Social competence is generally inferior in these children compared with securely attached children. They are likely to have difficulty in their peer relationships and are less likely to have satisfying relationships.

These children tend not to seek comfort when upset. They lack trust in others and don't believe others will look after them. They tend to have high expectations that they should rely only on themselves and may find it hard to understand and manage their emotions. They tend to be critical of others.

Parental behaviour that may lead to avoidant attachment

Just as there are things you can do to encourage a secure attachment with your child, certain other behaviours may lead to an insecure attachment relationship.

Ignoring your child's distress

This shows your child that he will not receive help with his emotions and that his emotions don't matter. It shows your child that he has to deal with his own negative emotions. Children can become very distressed and find it hard to calm themselves. Children who don't receive support may try to suppress their feelings, and when they can no longer do that, there is likely to be an emotional outburst. You may not have been aware of the bottling process and so you are surprised by the intensity of emotion that your child is showing. Because the intensity seems exaggerated, you may be even less inclined to offer support because you might worry about encouraging your child to have such displays. However, the evidence shows that children who have their emotions responded to, have fewer outbursts and less distress than children who are ignored when they are upset.

Harsh responses to distress

Children who are yelled at or criticised when they are upset are also more likely to become insecurely attached.

Hostility/anger towards your child

Children who in their daily interactions with their parents bear the brunt of their parent's anger and hostility may become insecurely attached and feel emotionally unsafe.

Intrusive parenting

Intrusive parenting is when a parent doesn't give their child the psychological space they need. Everyone needs time to themselves. Parents may be intrusive by over-stimulating a child, or not reading his signals that he needs time to himself.

Avoidant attachment in adulthood

Avoidantly attached adults want to depend on themselves. They feel a sense of shame if they need others and believe they should be self-sufficient. They feel they should be able to manage everything without anyone's assistance. They tend to be worried about others getting too close to them and feel uncomfortable about intimacy. Discomfort with their feelings, and especially disclosing their feelings, can interfere with getting support and enjoying relationships. They are prone to relationship difficulties, both in romantic ties and friendships. They are less likely to accept their partner's faults. Their perception of the world is that it is an unpredictable place where their needs won't be met. Reactions to stress and its association with attachment style have been researched. As stress increases, these adults become less likely to seek support. Also, as stress increases for a partner of an avoidantly attached adult, they are less likely to provide support. In the work setting, these people tend to want to keep busy and prefer to avoid interacting with others.

Anxious attachment

Emilio is a three-year-old with an anxious attachment to his mother. He is very clingy and cries often. His mother found it hard to be consistent because of disruptions and stress in her own life. Sometimes she could meet his needs, while at other times she couldn't. Emilio acts like he wants his mother's comfort as he follows her around and wants to be picked up, but then he responds angrily to her efforts to calm him down. He attends three-year-old kinder, but cries when he is dropped off. He doesn't cope well with the demands of the program and fights with other children.

The anxious attachment relationship is characterised by tension and distress for both the child and parent (about 10 percent of children fall into this category). Emotions are not dealt with, especially negative emotions. When a child is upset or angry, tension escalates in both the parent and child, and there is a lack of effective soothing. Both parent and child feel frustrated by the relationship. The child is trying to obtain comfort, yet is also resisting parental efforts to soothe.

Using you as a secure base

Anxious attachment means that a child is unable to use his parent as a secure base because he is not confident he will receive help when he needs it. Children who are anxiously attached find it very hard to separate from their parent. Some separation anxiety is normal, though, and does not necessarily mean the child is insecurely attached.

Effects on your child

An anxiously attached child is often distressed. Efforts to soothe this child often seem in vain, and he continues to cry. He tends to be clingy (all children are clingy to some extent) and anxious about being left alone. He tends to have low self-esteem, feelings of incompetence and insecurity. He is prone to difficulties coping with stressful situations, and is at risk for developing anxiety, depression and behaviour problems.

The anxiously attached child is also more vulnerable to becoming a victim of bullying than a securely attached child. He may be clingy towards teachers and other caregivers, and lack confidence with peers.

He is likely to see himself as unlovable and feel anxious about whether others will meet his needs.

Parental behaviour that may lead to anxious attachment

Responding inconsistently to distress. Depending on how the parent is feeling, he or she might be sympathetic and attempt to soothe the child when he is upset. At other times, however, the parent ignores the child's cries and bids for attention. So there is oscillation between being attentive and ignoring the child.

Being sarcastic. The parent is often angry and frustrated with the child, and speaks in a harsh tone, at times using sarcasm, ridicule and criticism.

Anxious attachment in adulthood

Adult relationships tend to be fraught with jealousy and fears of abandonment, and a wish for excessive intimacy and over-involvement with people. People with anxious attachment tend to have high levels of distress and difficulty managing their emotions. Other people may be idealised or denigrated (or both, in succession).

Disoriented/disorganised attachment

There is less research on this more recently formulated category of attachment than the other categories outlined. It is a type of insecure attachment where a child may display puzzling and contradictory behaviours. He may appear dazed and confused. This attachment style is associated with parental behaviour that frightens children. Examples of such behaviour include abuse, looking scared, handling the child roughly, or asking the child to comfort them when the parent is upset. These children have not had their needs met in a consistent and sensitive manner.

QUALITY OF DAILY CARE

The quality of a child's attachment to his caregiver is highly dependent on the quality of care that the child experiences in his daily life. This means that you can do a lot to promote secure attachment.

IT WON'T HAPPEN OVERNIGHT ...

Attachment develops over time. It does not happen instantly at birth, or at any other time, for that matter. It is a gradual unfolding and developing of a relationship. All relationships have good and bad days. Attachment is determined by overall care, not one-off events.

CONTINUITY OVER GENERATIONS

There tends to be some continuity in the style of attachment across generations. Parents who have a secure attachment to their own parents are likely to foster secure attachment in their own child. However, there are things you can do to break the pattern of handing down insecure attachment. An important aspect is to come to terms with your own attachment history. Parents with insecure attachment to their own parents who have insight into this have a better chance of fostering secure attachment in their child than parents who have not come to terms with their history.

QUALITY OF ATTACHMENT CAN CHANGE

Because quality of attachment is dependent on parenting, if parenting changes then the quality of attachment can change. For example, severe stress in a family can reduce the quality of care provided to a child. If this is prolonged, there is a risk that a securely attached child may become insecurely attached. Likewise, an insecurely attached child who goes on to experience positive and consistent parenting may become securely attached.

A POSITIVE INFLUENCE

It is not only parent–child relationships that matter. A secure attachment might be formed with an aunt or grandfather. A secure attachment with anyone makes a child more resilient (better able to cope with stress and overcome difficulties). It is encouraging to know that positive relationships can make up for previously negative relationships. A child with a secure attachment to one parent is better off than a child with insecure attachments to both parents, but of course the ideal scenario is to have secure attachments to both parents.

Even a child with no secure attachments in childhood may form a secure attachment in adolescence or adulthood. It is possible for adults who have a history of insecure attachment to establish secure attachments in adulthood, for example with a partner. This secure attachment can help the person to form new beliefs about themselves (e.g. that they are loveable and worthy of care) and others (that they can be trusted). This can help the person to overcome the effects of their insecure attachment history. Their new experiences can help them to parent in a manner that promotes secure attachment in their own children, rather than perpetuating insecure attachment.

WHAT ABOUT MY CHILD'S TEMPERAMENT?

Temperament refers to characteristics of personality that are believed to be inborn and biologically based. A child's level of activity, flexibility and sociability are some commonly measured temperament traits. Children who have temperaments that make them more difficult to look after (e.g. babies who cry easily) place more demands on their parents' time and energy.

Secure attachment develops with responsive and warm parenting. If your child is cranky and cries easily, it might test your patience and make it hard for you to be responsive and warm. Your child's temperament can make it harder for you to provide the care that your child needs. Quality of care is still the main determinant of attachment security, but a child with a 'difficult' temperament requires more care.

Some research has found that children with a 'difficult' temperament developed secure attachment if their parents received support that allowed them to provide good quality care, while those parents without support found it hard to provide the same quality of care, and therefore the risk of insecure attachment increased.

'GOODNESS OF FIT'

Researchers who speak of temperament often mention the idea of 'goodness of fit'. Basically this means that different children need different parenting. A child who cries easily will need more soothing than a child who does not. By altering parenting responses to take into account the child's temperament, the parent is shaping their care to meet the child's needs.

MEETING YOUR CHILD'S EMOTIONAL NEEDS

Just as nutritional needs are met through regular, healthy food intake, so emotional needs are met through day-to-day interactions with others. Children's emotional needs are met through supportive and understanding interactions with their parents and other significant figures in their lives such as grandparents, relatives, carers, siblings.

Sometimes people artificially divide the parenting tasks of setting limits and meeting the child's emotional needs. However, all parenting impacts on your child's emotional state because his emotions are ever-present (as is the case with adults). Ideally, you will be mindful of your child's emotional needs regardless of what aspect of parenting you are engaged in, be it reprimanding your child for his behaviour, having a conversation or showing affection. This does not mean that your child's emotions should necessarily take precedence over other issues. For example, just because a child is upset about going to bed does not mean that he should be allowed to stay up. However, by keeping in mind your child's emotional state, you can consider how best to meet your objective. For example, if your child feels guilty about a misdemeanour, you may reprimand him more gently than you would otherwise, because your child may otherwise be overburdened with guilty feelings and not be able to listen to what you are saying.

It is through ordinary, day-to-day interactions that you meet your child's emotional needs. During daily events such as getting ready for school, helping with homework and family outings you interact with your child, and these interactions impact on his emotional state. Emotional needs are not something that can be taken out on a Saturday afternoon for addressing, and then packed away for convenience during the rest of the week. Trying to be mindful of your child's emotional needs in daily life is one of the key challenges of meeting his emotional needs.

VERBAL AND NONVERBAL COMMUNICATION

You communicate with your child both verbally and nonverbally. Verbal communication is what you actually say. Nonverbal communication includes facial expressions, tone of voice, the way you look at your child, your physical movements (e.g. whether you are being gentle or rough). Nonverbal communication plays a large role in our interpretation of what people are trying to tell us. Sometimes there is a discrepancy between our verbal and nonverbal communication. In such a case, your child will generally find the nonverbal message more convincing. For example, you might say 'That painting looks great' in a cool tone of voice to your child. He will conclude that you are not really pleased with the picture. For a message to get through, your words have to match your actions. Words are only a small part of the communication process.

Children are sensitive to what their parents are communicating and tend to assume that communication is directed at them (even when it is not). Your child will observe your behaviour, facial expression and moods. If you habitually scowl or are irritable, your child is likely to think that you are angry with him, even if your mood has nothing to do with him.

Because your child's emotional needs are met by the actions and messages – verbal and nonverbal – that you give in the course of daily life, you can relatively easily change the communication you are providing. Extra smiles, a ruffle of his hair, a quick hug, a warm tone of voice, can do an enormous amount for your child's sense of security and can be easily fitted into daily life.

YOUR CHILD'S ENVIRONMENT – SEEING THE WHOLE PICTURE

Your child's emotional development is affected by his experiences in all environments – at home, crèche, with extended family, school and other places he goes.

The two steps in meeting your child's emotional needs involve:

1. interacting with your child in a way that meets his emotional needs, and avoiding interactions that undermine his emotional health. You might be pleased with how you

interact with your child 60 percent of the time. But for the other 40 percent of the time, you might be critical or dismissive of him. The effect of the positive interactions can be washed away by the negative interactions, so consistency of positive interactions is important.

2. considering the wider environment that your child is exposed to. What is happening between him and other members of the family? Is your child being bullied at school (or home)? What is the emotional climate at home?

Factors that influence your child's emotional health

★ interactions with extended family members, especially if he spends considerable time in their care – are the interactions supportive of your child?

★ interactions with siblings – is there excessive fighting or bullying behaviour?

★ the emotional climate at home – is there tension or a relaxed climate?

★ conflict at home – are there arguments, yelling or domestic violence?

★ quality of peer interactions at school

★ lack of routine

★ whether your child is in a child-appropriate setting – is he protected from inappropriate material, e.g. violent videos and disturbing images?

★ is he getting enough sleep?

★ is he eating a balanced diet?

★ physical health (e.g. diabetes can influence mood, while low iron levels can make your child lethargic and less able to cope with the demands of daily life).

When considering the above list of factors, we all have biases. It can be easier to believe something is going wrong at school than at home. Of course, there may be a combination of factors that are influencing your child's emotions.

Summary

The seven key emotional needs of children are:

▶ to have a secure attachment

▶ to receive help with emotional regulation

▶ to receive support

▶ to have a sense of belonging

▶ to feel loved

▶ to feel your approval

▶ to have a clear understanding of expectations, routines and boundaries.

These needs are about day-to-day interactions and require your involvement.

Emotional development

3

Faye, a four-month-old baby, cries easily; Harry, a two-year-old, throws tantrums; and Brad, a ten-year-old, is able to speak clearly about his feelings (for example, that he felt disappointed when he lost the hockey grand final). What is responsible for these changes in emotional experiences and expression? Just as children grow physically and develop skills like walking and running, children also develop emotionally.

Emotional development starts from birth. Babies experience emotions from the time they are born (possibly even before birth), including distress and contentment.

WHAT CHANGES OCCUR DURING EMOTIONAL DEVELOPMENT?

Three main changes occur as your child develops emotionally:

1. the range of feelings she experiences broadens

2. her ability to recognise her own and other people's feelings increases

3. her ability to regulate her own emotions improves.

The range of feelings

Initially, babies experience distress and contentment. It is difficult to know for sure what your baby actually feels, but during her first year of life, the range of feelings she experiences broadens to include fear, anger, excitement, and so on. Somewhere around eighteen months, she will start to experience more complex emotions that depend on awareness of social rules, such as pride, shame and embarrassment. By the age of eighteen months, she may experience the entire range of emotions that adults do.

Recognising feelings

Babies are affected by adults' facial and verbal expressions of emotion, so at some level babies must be able to recognise adults' feelings. When adults interact with babies with a blank or unhappy facial expression (in some studies parents are suffering depression; in other studies parents are asked to purposely put on blank or sad facial expressions), babies get upset, or look away and don't play as much. In contrast, when adults show happy facial expressions and tone of voice, babies respond positively, are more likely to be happy themselves, play better, seem keen to interact with the adult, and enjoy the interaction.

When a child begins to talk, she soon starts referring to her own feelings, and other people's feelings. Her conversations suggest that she understands that people's emotions can be caused by specific events, e.g. 'Harry was sad at kinder because he lost his toy.' She may even be able to predict how someone will feel depending on the situation they are experiencing. Children also show an understanding that people's behaviour can be caused by feelings, e.g. 'The boy is hiding because he's scared of the dog.' During her primary school years, a child develops the understanding that people can have mixed emotions (e.g. feeling scared and excited at the same time about going on an amusement ride).

Recognising her own feelings is an important first step for your child in developing strategies for coping with emotions. Is she angry or disappointed or jealous? Does she feel happy? Depending on what she is feeling, different coping strategies may be helpful.

The ability to regulate emotions

Babies are nearly totally dependent on their caregivers to regulate their emotions. If your baby is not soothed when upset, she will continue to cry for some time. Eventually, she might fall asleep from exhaustion, but she is not equipped to manage her feelings. Your baby does have some basic abilities to try to soothe herself, such as sucking, but often these are not sufficient to calm her.

Children learn how to calm themselves by receiving soothing from their caregivers. Given a supportive environment, your child will gradually learn emotional regulation skills. A child grows emotionally from near total dependence on carers for emotional regulation to some independence in managing her own emotions. This process is gradual and occurs over years. Children who are not soothed by others can have problems regulating their emotions that may persist into adolescence and adulthood. There are adults who become easily upset, who experience intense anger or sadness, and who don't have healthy strategies to calm themselves.

VARYING DEGREES OF EMOTIONAL NEED

Children vary in the amount of emotional support they require in daily life. The level of support a child needs changes as she matures, and it also changes from day to day depending on what is happening.

The level of support a child needs depends on several factors.

Child's age

Children in infancy and toddlerhood require particularly high levels of help with emotional regulation – they may need help every few moments on a difficult day.

Child's temperament

Some children cry more easily than others and find it harder to calm down. These children require extra amounts of soothing to help regulate their emotions, otherwise they spend a lot of their time crying.

Level of stress

If a child is stressed because of changes (e.g. starting a new crèche or school; the birth of a sibling; moving house) she is likely to be upset more easily and may need more support and nurturing during this time. If a child is not given the extra assistance when she needs it, her problems with emotional regulation may persist long after the stressful event has subsided.

Physical sickness or tiredness

When children feel physically unwell or tired they are generally more vulnerable to becoming upset and are likely to find it harder to calm down. So extra emotional support may be needed when your child is physically depleted.

THE BENEFITS OF EMOTIONAL REGULATION

Children whose parents help them with emotional regulation are better able to reach their potential, to have harmonious social relationships, and to experience wellbeing. In contrast, children whose emotions are not well managed are disadvantaged in many ways. For example, a child may not be able to do her schoolwork because she is too excited to concentrate. A child may have peer relationship problems because she has trouble managing her anger, and lashes out at people. A child who is often angry or upset wastes a lot of time being in a negative emotional state. It is wasted time because she is not exploring her surroundings, or observing what is going on around her, or having fun playing, or interacting positively with her parents, brothers or sisters, or friends. Of course, everyone has times when they are not happy – this is an inevitable part of life. Parents who try to help their child regulate her emotions can maximise the time that she feels content. This can benefit the child's behaviour, emotional development and relationships.

WHAT STAYS THE SAME DURING EMOTIONAL DEVELOPMENT?

There are some things that will remain constant through your child's emotional development, so they will hold true regardless of her age.

The need to receive emotional support

Whether your child is three months or eleven years, she needs emotional support. This need continues throughout adolescence and adulthood. How often a child needs support varies – as your child gets older she is likely to need soothing less often. The most appropriate way to give support also varies as the child gets older – a baby may need to be carried, while an eight-year-old child may need physical affection, as well as talking, to help her calm down.

Emotions are an important part of wellbeing

Emotional health matters a great deal, whether your child is in her infancy, a toddler, or in primary school.

The importance of secure attachment

The need to have a secure attachment with parents (or other caregivers) remains, regardless of your child's age.

HOW DO ADULTS AND CHILDREN DIFFER IN THEIR EMOTIONAL EXPERIENCES?

A major difference between adults and children is how easily they get upset. Children get upset more easily than adults. Let's consider the issue of physical comfort. Why don't adults burst into tears when they are physically uncomfortable? The main reasons are that adults have better developed reasoning skills and emotional regulation skills.

Reasoning skills

Babies don't have the same sense of past, present and future as adults do, and it is likely that babies experience the present like it is all there is. Your baby doesn't have the reasoning skills to figure out that an uncomfortable feeling (e.g. hunger, a wet nappy, feeling cold) will end. You know that the discomfort will pass (e.g. an adult who is cold walking from the car to the shop knows the discomfort is only momentary).

Emotional regulation skills

A baby lying in a cot doesn't have the advantage of emotional regulation strategies. She feels hungry and there appears to be no end in sight – she feels overwhelmed and cries. You generally know that there are things you can do to change the situation if you feel uncomfortable (put on a jumper, get a glass of water to cool down). An adult is aware of resources available to them and what coping strategies can be used to make the situation better. You can engage in many forms of emotional regulation. Talking to someone when you feel down, using calming self-talk (e.g. 'it's going to be fine'), going for a jog to relieve tension, listening to your favourite music – all these can help to change how you feel or help you to cope with your feelings.

EMOTIONAL REGULATION

There are two aspects to emotional regulation:

1. the level of distress that your child is experiencing on an ongoing basis

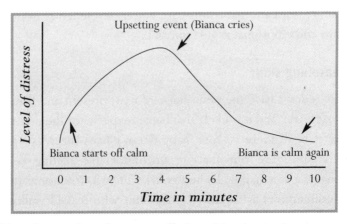

'Normal' emotional state. Bianca starts off calm, and then there is a distressing event. She gets upset, but recovers within minutes and returns to a calm state.

2. how quickly she recovers from an emotional upset.

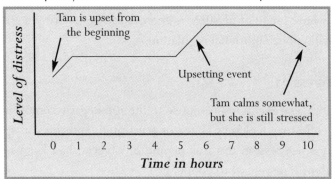

Ongoing emotional distress. Even before an upsetting event, Tam is emotionally distressed – but it is not obvious from looking at her. She looks calm, but inside she is harbouring feelings of anger and irritation. When an upsetting event happens, Tam's reaction looks 'over the top'. But when her ongoing level of distress is considered, it makes sense that she is so upset. When she calms down, she doesn't return to a 'normal' state, but rather to her previous level of irritability.

WHAT DOES POOR EMOTIONAL REGULATION LOOK LIKE?

★ flying off the handle

★ reacting instantly to provocation without thinking

★ poor ability to cope with frustration

★ when angry, finding it hard to calm down for a long time

★ reacting to minor provocation (e.g. getting angry because you are stuck in traffic).

Some of these indicators of poor emotional regulation are seen in normal development. Your toddler is upset easily and generally reacts quickly without seeming to think through the situation. That is why she needs so much help from you. If your child receives the support she needs, she is likely to develop healthy coping strategies to deal with her emotions.

The results of poor emotional regulation

A whole range of negative outcomes can result from a child having poor emotional regulation.

Aggression

Often aggression is a response to intense negative emotions. A child may feel very angry or frustrated, and this can spill out as aggression towards people or objects, bad language, rudeness or refusal to cooperate.

Inability to calm themselves

If a child has poor emotional regulation, she may be distressed for a long time. A child who has poor emotional regulation skills has difficulty calming herself after upsetting events. In essence, she finds it hard to 'get over' the upsetting incident. For example, if a child's feelings have been hurt, is she able to do things to make herself feel better? Does she find someone to talk to for understanding, comfort and reassurance or try to understand what motivated the person (e.g. maybe they were in a bad mood)? If a child takes a long time to calm down, this can interfere with her wellbeing, relationships and behaviour and may be related to mental health problems such as depression, anxiety and behavioural disorders.

Impaired social relationships

A child with poor emotional regulation is likely to show aggression to peers. She may be frequently upset by interactions that occur as a usual part of social interaction, e.g. having to wait her turn. She may seem inconsiderate because she is too preoccupied with her emotional state to consider how other people are feeling. As a result, the child may be unpopular and have unsatisfactory relationships.

Poor coping ability

Part of coping with most events in life relies on being able to manage our emotional reaction to situations that we find ourselves in. If emotions are not managed, your child's ability to cope with situations is compromised. For example, test anxiety interferes with a child's ability to demonstrate what they have learnt. A child with test anxiety may actually have learnt the material very well, but because she is not able to manage her feelings of anxiety, her ability to perform is seriously compromised. Given that so many academic tasks, competitive sport, scholarship and music examinations depend on 'test' situations, your child may feel the full impact of not being able to manage her emotions.

Interference with task completion

To complete tasks at home and school, your child needs to be able to concentrate. It is well known that emotions easily interfere with concentration. Feelings of anxiety, depression, and even excitement all serve to reduce your child's ability to concentrate. The ability to manage both positive and negative emotions is important for being able to complete tasks such as homework and chores. Another important aspect of task completion is the ability to delay gratification. Many tasks have boring parts to them. Your child might be bored by her maths sums or by setting the table. She needs to be able to persevere and manage her feeling of boredom to complete the tasks (adults may have this challenge too!).

The ability to empathise

The ability to understand someone else's feelings and motivations, and to care about their emotional state, is called empathy. Empathy emerges early in life. A child between twelve and eighteen months starts to show concern about others' feelings. For example, she might become upset if another child is upset, and she may offer a tissue or give the person a hug. Some would argue that it is just 'emotional contagion' – that the child is affected by someone else's feelings without understanding that there is someone else experiencing those feelings. There is evidence, however, that children in their first few years of life do understand that others have needs, wishes, desires, and feelings. As your child's reasoning skills improve and she is more able to consider things from another perspective, she becomes more proficient in thinking about other people's emotional experiences. Empathy is important for social and family relationships. It helps your child to develop solid and meaningful relationships with peers and adults. When a child soothes another child who has grazed her knee or a crying child who misses his mum, a child is demonstrating empathy. Empathy continues to be important throughout childhood and adulthood.

The vast majority of children have the capacity for empathy. (Children with developmental disorders such as autism, which prevent them from feeling empathy, are a rare exception.)

Factors that influence a child's development of empathy

★ *The extent to which parents (and carers) show empathy towards the child.* A child who receives empathy as part of their daily care is much more likely to develop empathy towards other people.

★ *The emotional arousal of a child.* If a child is angry or upset, there is less chance she will empathise in a particular situation. It is hard to think about other people's feelings if our own feelings are overwhelming us.

★ *The extent to which caregivers help the child to focus on the other person's feelings.* Parents and caregivers can talk to children about other people's feelings and this is likely to help them to develop empathy. (But just talking to a child about empathy, without showing her empathy when she is upset is not likely to work.)

★ *The child's overall level of emotional health.* Children who are securely attached and generally happy are more likely to empathise with others. Children who are insecurely attached, or anxious, depressed or angry, generally find it *more difficult to empathise.*

So, what are the possible results of a lack of empathy?

Antisocial behaviour

A strong motivator for positive social behaviour (such as sharing or helping others) is empathy. Empathy allows us to consider how our actions might impact on others. A lack of understanding of other people's views and feelings is often related to aggressive or inconsiderate behaviour.

Impaired relationships

Part of empathy involves understanding how other people feel and think. Lack of empathy cuts a child off from others' experiences and feelings. This can impair the quality of relationships she has. To have a mutually caring relationship, your child needs to give and receive empathy so that genuine understanding can occur.

Milestones in emotional development

Here are some milestones in children's emotional development.

Birth to one year

★ Experiencing a wide range of emotions such as happiness, anger, fear, and contentment.

★ Forming an attachment relationship. Babies who are well looked after will develop trust in their caregivers – and will develop secure attachment relationships. A baby who receives inconsistent or inadequate care tends to cry more, and may be withdrawn and unresponsive to people and her environment.

★ Social interactions like maintaining eye contact with caregivers and cooing or making other sounds.

★ Responding to the emotional tone of caregivers' interactions.

★ Stranger anxiety emerges usually some time between seven and twelve months.

One to four years

★ Self-conscious emotions emerge – e.g. pride, embarrassment.

★ Able to talk about her own and other people's feelings.

★ Empathy for other people emerges.

★ Starts to develop strategies for emotional regulation – e.g. talking to herself for reassurance ('mum will be back soon'). They can nonetheless still be very dependent on adults for help with emotional regulation.

Five to twelve years

★ Greater ability to discuss her emotions.

★ More able to regulate her emotions, therefore fewer tantrums, and when she does get upset, she is more able to calm herself.

★ Her emotions tend to be more stable (not the sudden changes often seen in toddlerhood).

★ Increased ability to empathise with others, and to consider the effects of her behaviour on other people.

★ Able to understand that a person can have a few emotions at the same time, e.g. feeling scared and excited.

THE COMMUNICATION OF EMOTION

Your child will have different capacities to communicate at different ages. A child's ability to express herself verbally, to reason and to be aware of her feelings, all change a great deal as she matures. A child at the age of three or four years can seem bright and may understand many aspects of this world. Yet when it comes to discussing or regulating her feelings, she may really struggle. This can be puzzling for you because you see your child being so competent in one area, and it's easy to assume it extends to other areas.

Babies

★ Babies have a limited ability to communicate.

★ Crying is the most common way that babies show that they are upset. A baby might cry because she is in pain, hungry, lonely or uncomfortable – she can't communicate exactly what she needs or wants, but her cries show clearly that something is wrong!

★ Facial expressions. Grimacing, or a blank, sad facial expression can also show a baby's feelings. Smiling shows happiness and can be a signal your baby wants to communicate with others. Eye contact can also be an effort to communicate.

★ Body movements. A baby might arch her back in discomfort, or wriggle about in excitement.

★ Vocalisation. A child might grunt with frustration, or squeal with delight. Cooing sounds can be some of your baby's first efforts at social communication.

Toddlers

★ Often toddlers express their feelings through their behaviour.

★ Indirect communication of feelings is common: e.g. whingeing because she is unhappy; crying at separation because she is scared (but not saying that directly).

★ Toddlers are gradually more able to express their emotions verbally.

★ At times of high emotional intensity, a toddler's ability to report what she is feeling declines, and she is more likely to show disturbed behaviour, e.g. if very scared, she might scream and cling, but most probably wouldn't say she is scared.

★ For you to understand your toddler's emotions you need to be paying attention to your child's behaviour for clues.

Children aged five to twelve years

★ Children of this age have a better ability to talk about their emotions, but can still find it difficult to do so.

★ Facial expressions can be an important source of information.

★ Changes in behaviour can signal changes in feelings. During the toddler years, behaviour indicating upset can be very obvious – while during the primary school years, children may show subtle changes – your child may become less talkative if she is worried; or more irritable if she is upset about something. Careful observation can help you to figure out how your child is feeling.

YOUR ROLE IN HELPING YOUR CHILD DEVELOP EMOTIONALLY

Parents play a key role in children's emotional development. A big influence on your child's emotional development is the consistency and quality of care that is provided to her within the home, and the type of experiences she has (e.g. positive experiences such as family picnics, receiving affection, or negative experiences such as exposure to violent video games, exposure to family violence). The care your child receives in the broader community (e.g. childcare, kindergarten and school) also affects her emotional development. By meeting your child's emotional needs, you increase her wellbeing and help her to learn emotional regulation skills and to develop empathy for other people. When you meet your child's emotional needs you are fostering resilience in your child.

Helping your child regulate her emotions

★ Meet your child's emotional needs for emotional security, approval, and so on.

★ Actively help your child with emotional regulation. Don't expect her to be independent in managing her emotions.

★ Empathise with your child. It is a powerful influence in helping your child develop empathy for others.

WHAT IS EMOTIONAL HEALTH?

Just as we can talk about a child being sick or healthy in a physical sense, we can also talk about health in an emotional sense. When a child has a physical sickness, it interferes with her life. She might not be able to attend school or enjoy riding her bike. Her quality of life is diminished. Thankfully in most cases this is only for a few days. Emotional health stems from your child having her emotional needs met – just as good nutrition is vital for physical health.

Meeting emotional needs does not 'spoil' a child; rather it gives her the best chance of growing up happy and well adjusted. Emotional health relates to every part of your child's functioning. Is she sociable? Can she make and keep friends? Does she know how to behave appropriately in different situations? Is she able to learn and pay attention at school? Can she be depended on to do tasks that need to be done, and to cooperate in the family? Is she happy? All these questions relate, either directly or indirectly, to your child's emotional health.

Emotional development is a process that occurs gradually over time. Some things that are considered normal at one stage of development may be of serious concern at another. For example, a three-year-old throwing herself on the floor with anger is not unusual. If a thirteen-year-old did the same, it would be a cause for concern.

Age	Signs of emotional health
Birth to one year	• Usually able to be soothed when crying • Smiles and shows enjoyment in social interactions (some of the time)
One to four years	• Interested in various activities • Can use parents as a secure base if upset • Able to be calmed down in a reasonable amount of time (e.g. within minutes rather than hours) • Recovers reasonably quickly from upset
Five to twelve years	• Seems content most of the time • Smiles and laughs regularly • Is interested in a variety of things • Can be angry in response to specific events (e.g. someone has taken her belongings) but usually not angry without provocation • Seems reasonably stable emotionally (not experiencing wild mood swings) • Shows empathy for other people • Often shows care towards family, friends, and animals.

Summary

▶ Your child experiences a range of emotions from the time she is born.

▶ Your child needs a lot of assistance from her caregivers to manage her emotions.

▶ The emotional development tasks for your child are to gain a sense of emotional security, the ability to manage her emotions, and to develop empathy for others.

▶ Your child's emotional development is closely linked to the care that she receives in her daily life.

The importance of parental empathy

To have a positive parent–child relationship, you need to have empathy for your child. When you empathise with your child, you see the world from his perspective. Empathy can help you to know what your child needs, how to best reason with your child, and how to comfort him. Empathy gives you a window into your child's psychological world.

WHAT IS EMPATHY?

Empathy has three aspects: understanding another person's perspective, your feelings about the situation, and your actions towards the person.

Understanding

A key part of empathy is understanding how your child feels and thinks, and what emotions or motivations underpin his behaviour in a particular situation.

Feelings

When you empathise, you are likely to feel concern about your child's wellbeing (or to be happy for him if he has had a positive experience). Either way, your emotions are likely to be focused on your child's needs. In contrast, when you don't empathise, you tend to have feelings that are focused on yourself (for example, feeling irritated that you are being imposed upon).

Actions

When parents empathise they are motivated to help their child (if the child is distressed), for example by reassuring the child, or helping him problem solve.

Empathising with your child does not mean that he will necessarily get what he wants. For example, your child may be anxious about going to school. Empathising with your child should not mean that you let him stay home. Rather, you may be supportive and reassuring, but he would still have to go. Likewise, you may empathise with your child's wish to have ice cream before dinner, but it doesn't mean that you give it to him.

Why empathise?

★ You are less likely to misinterpret your child's behaviour (e.g. thinking that your child is asking for ice cream because he is difficult rather than because he is hungry).

★ You will understand what is happening for your child (e.g. not wanting to go to school because of anxiety, or because he hasn't done his homework). When you understand your child, it puts you in the best position to know how to help him. If your child is worried about not having done his homework, you could try to help him be more organised. If there are friendship problems, you might speak to his teacher. So even though your child still goes to school, empathy helps you to help your child. It also influences how you might help your child to go to school (in a supportive way). If you think your child is being manipulative you might criticise or berate him, making him feel even worse.

★ Empathy motivates you to provide your child with the emotional support he needs. If your child is crying for the third time in an hour, you need to empathise to have the inclination to be supportive yet again. Without empathy, you are likely to think your child is being unreasonable and may be trying to control the situation with his crying. This belief is likely to prevent you from being supportive and helping your child with his emotions.

THE EMPATHY PROCESS

Jenny is four years old. Her two-year-old sister has just taken her favourite doll.
Parent's perspective: *No big deal. We share in this family.*
Jenny's perspective: *This is a disaster. It's my doll and I want it back!*

What is likely to happen if Jenny's parent empathises with her?

Understanding If Jenny's parent empathises, he or she will see that Jenny is really upset about this. It is hard for Jenny to share something she likes so much. Her parent might think: 'I need to help Jenny deal with her feelings and the situation.'

Feelings Understanding that Jenny is upset, her parent is likely to feel concerned for her. 'I know you love the doll and it must be hard for you to lend it …'.

Action Jenny's parent might talk soothingly to her and try to find a solution. 'It's okay, your sister will give it back in a moment. Why don't you play with the other doll while you are waiting?'

The effect on Jenny

Jenny is likely to feel her parent is listening to her and considering her perspective. This is likely to help her to calm down and think about the situation. The cooperative approach her parent has taken is likely to make Jenny more open to sharing. Of course, Jenny may not be easy to distract and she may continue to be upset, but a calm reassuring approach by her parent is likely to help her and, at the very least, it won't make her feel worse.

LACK OF THE EMPATHY PROCESS

What is likely to happen if Jenny's parent does not empathise with her?

Understanding If her parent doesn't understand what is happening from Jenny's point of view, they may think: 'Jenny is over-reacting and is being selfish. She is trying to get attention with her difficult behaviour. I need to show Jenny that her bad behaviour will not be rewarded. Also, I have told her many times she needs to share; she has obviously not been listening to me.'

Feelings This negative interpretation of what is going on may lead to Jenny's parent feeling annoyed and angry that Jenny is 'misbehaving'. The parent is focused on Jenny's behaviour rather than her feelings.

Action Leading on from this negative interpretation and feelings of irritation, Jenny's parent is likely to respond in a way that doesn't help Jenny deal with the situation. For example, he or she may tell Jenny to stop being silly and that if she can't share, she will have her doll taken away from her.

The effect on Jenny

Jenny is likely to feel that her parent is not listening to her and that this is unfair. She is likely to feel more desperate about the fact that she has lost possession of the doll to her little sister. Most likely, she is no closer to learning how to share.

EMOTIONAL CONTAGION IS NOT EMPATHY

We've all had the experience: someone is laughing and you start giggling, but you don't really know why. Likewise, someone might cry and you start to feel sad without even knowing why that person is crying. Emotional contagion is like 'catching' someone's emotion. That is not empathy. Your child is angry that he can't have ice cream, and now you are angry too. This interferes with your ability to consider your child's perspective. You start with one angry person, now there are two! It is likely that your feelings will be focused on yourself. And your actions are likely to be aimed at reducing your anger, not helping your child regulate his anger.

Similarly, let's consider anxiety. Your child is anxious about going to school. You can see it in his eyes. All of a sudden, you start to worry. What if someone picks on him? What if he gets lost? What if his teacher is not kind? You have experienced emotional contagion (you've 'caught' the feeling of anxiety). Now it is hard to think about what your child is thinking or feeling, because you are having strong feelings of worry. Your face and your actions will show your child that you are worried. This increases your child's worry (there must be something to worry about if mum/dad is looking pale!). You will probably act in a way that increases his worry rather than giving him confidence and reassurance.

Empathy is about understanding how your child is feeling without being swamped by the same feeling yourself. Of course, you may feel some of their emotion; if you know they are sad, you might feel somewhat sad yourself. But when you feel swamped by the emotion, it interferes with your ability to empathise. It makes it hard to step back and consider what is going on for your child and to remain calm and clear-headed enough to help him deal with the situation and his feelings.

TYPES OF PARENT–CHILD RELATIONSHIPS AND EMPATHY

Broadly, we can categorise parent–child relationships into three categories: too close (enmeshment), distant, and healthy closeness. In a parent–child relationship that is too close or too distant, it can be hard for the parent to empathise.

Too close – 'enmeshment'

Enmeshment is when a parent and child are too close. The reason it is unhealthy is that the parent has difficulty seeing their child as separate from themselves. A lot of emotional contagion happens in enmeshed relationships; your child may be anxious, and then you become anxious too. Or you may feel happy about something and believe your child actually feels happy about it, when in fact he may not. There is a difficulty in separating which emotions belong to you and which emotions belong to your child. This type of relationship is an impediment to empathy because in order to empathise, you need to recognise that your child is a separate individual. Your feelings are not necessarily your child's feelings. Another feature of enmeshment is that your child is not given the psychological space he needs to have his own experiences and to develop an appropriate amount of independence.

Distant

In a distant parent–child relationship, there is not much communication about the child's feelings. This reduces a parent's ability to empathise because the information needed to form an empathic position is missing. In a distant relationship, parents may feel an emotional distance between themselves and their child, and may find it is hard to understand him.

Healthy closeness

In a parent–child relationship where there is a healthy closeness, the parent is able to think of the child as a separate person with his own experiences (which may or may not correspond with their own). A healthy closeness means you are supportive of your child, and are able to provide care based on what he needs. Empathy requires you to see your child as a separate person who has his own experiences, but also to feel in touch with your child's moods and experiences.

EMPATHY AND YOUR CHILD'S EMOTIONAL NEEDS

To meet your child's emotional needs you need to know what your child is feeling. You may say or do different things depending on whether your child is sad, angry or feeling left out. If you don't know how your child feels, your actions are likely to miss the mark.

How your beliefs about your child affect your empathy

Your level of empathy is influenced by your beliefs about your child. We all hold beliefs about people we know – family, friends and acquaintances. The beliefs we have about people relate to what kind of person we believe someone is. Likewise, parents have beliefs about their child. We are not always conscious of our beliefs and it is easy to mistake them for reality.

Beliefs tend to develop over time. Once established, beliefs can be hard to change. It is hard to talk yourself into believing something else about a person. We think, 'I'll believe it when I see it.' This attitude can be problematic, because your beliefs have a powerful impact on how you interact with someone (especially your child), and your interactions have a big influence on how your child responds. If the process is negative, your beliefs can be reinforced. For example, if you believe that your child is manipulative, you are likely to be suspicious of his motivation and respond in a defensive rather than supportive manner. This may upset your child and contribute to him misbehaving. This misbehaviour then reinforces your original belief that your child's motivation was askew. By changing your negative beliefs, you can break the negative cycle that may be occurring with your child.

Your beliefs about people in everyday life affect how you interpret what is going on. If you believe that your neighbour is helpful and then she lets you down, you are likely to think she must have had a good reason for it. Likewise, if you think your boss is mean and conniving and all of a sudden he is kind, you are likely to interpret his actions as having a malevolent motivation, or at least as insincere.

Similarly, your beliefs about your child influence your responses: are you supportive and understanding, or do you punish and criticise? Your actions affect your child emotionally and mentally. So if you start with negative beliefs, interpret your child's behaviour in a negative light and punish him, then your child's behaviour is likely to be difficult.

Negative beliefs

If you hold negative beliefs about your child, you may interpret your child's actions in such a way that he can't win. Often if your child is misbehaving or upset, you believe it reflects his true character. 'He is crying again because he always puts on a performance', or 'He is misbehaving because he only thinks about himself, and he doesn't care about what I say to him.' When your child is behaving well, or expressing affection toward you, you don't really believe your child means it. Sometimes you will see it as a manipulation to get what he wants. You may think: 'You only cleaned the table because you think that means I'll let you see your friends this afternoon', or 'You were good this morning, but as soon as you got what you wanted, you went back to your original self.'

PARENTS' BELIEFS

Parents' beliefs about their child will either help or get in the way of their empathy. Four beliefs are important for empathy.

1. My child is a good person.

2. My child is reasonable.

3. My child really feels the emotions he is showing (e.g. if he is crying, it means he must be upset).

4. My child is emotionally dependent on me (so my child is affected by what I say to him and the interactions between us).

On the other hand, there are beliefs that can reduce parents' empathy.

1. My child is hostile or manipulative.

2. My child is unreasonable.

3. My child is not really feeling the emotions he is showing, he is just putting on a show for attention.

4. My child is not emotionally dependent on me (what I do seems to have little or no effect on him).

Let us consider how each of these beliefs help or hinder parents' empathy.

1. My child has a good (or hostile) character

The belief that 'my child is hostile' interferes with empathy because the parent interprets events with the assumption that the child's motives are underpinned by malice. For example, a child starts crying and having a tantrum because he has to finish a game and go to bed. A parent who believes their child is hostile is likely to interpret such behaviour as, 'He is always testing the limits and refuses to listen to the rules. He thinks if he carries on loudly enough he will get what he wants', or 'His tantrum is an effort to manipulate the situation to get what he wants.' These negative interpretations focus the parent's mind on the child's behaviour rather than his feelings.

From the child's point of view, he is upset because he was having fun with the game and can't bear the idea of stopping it and going to bed (such things can be a big deal to a child). He is so overwhelmed by his emotions that he has a tantrum and cries. However, the parent only sees the 'bad' behaviour, not the distressed emotions fuelling the behaviour. The parent feels angry or irritated and responds by punishing the child or dismissing his feelings. The child does not have his emotional needs met, which in this case would consist of a soothing response to help him regain control of his feelings. Instead the child feels ignored (if the parent ignores his distress) or attacked (if he is punished) by his parent, which leads to increased distress. So he is likely to feel even more upset and his behaviour may escalate further (which then reinforces the parent's original belief that the child is indeed hostile).

Of course, the child does need to go to bed. A parent who empathises is able to enforce the rule, but in a supportive way. A parent who believes that their child has a good character (as opposed to a hostile one) may think that the child is finding it hard to finish the game because he is a child. Parents who believe their child has a good character generate explanations for their child's behaviour that assume the child's goodwill, for example interpreting misbehaviour as stemming from negative feelings, having a 'bad day', or other causes that do not reflect poorly on the child's character. The parent's response is likely to be supportive, while still enforcing the rule. For example, the parent might remind the child they can continue to play the game tomorrow. Or they may give an incentive for their child to go to bed (e.g. 'it will be warm and cosy and I'll read you a bedtime story'), and soothe the child by speaking to them kindly or giving them physical affection. Also, the parent is likely to give the child warnings before the game is finished (though of course, the child may still be upset even with plenty of notice). A supportive response is likely to make the child feel cared for and he is more likely to settle down. It is a win-win situation. The parent has maintained the rule (the child needs to go to bed so he gets enough sleep) while also being respectful of the child's feelings and the child has had his emotional needs met (in this case, being soothed and receiving comfort). So the parent's empathy allowed them to enforce the rule and meet the child's emotional needs. These two things are in no way contradictory.

If you feel swamped, it can be hard to step back and consider what is going on for your child, and to remain calm and clear-headed enough to help him deal with the situation and his feelings. The process of empathising can be demanding, but can make things easier in the long term because you are likely to feel more positive about your reactions to your child.

2. My child is (un)reasonable

The second belief that interferes with empathy is 'my child is unreasonable'. This puts a psychological distance between the parent and child because nobody sees themselves as unreasonable. If the parent believes their child is unreasonable they are likely to think that the child is behaving and reacting in ways that they would not do themselves. They conclude that they would not feel the same way as the child is feeling. The parent interprets events with the assumption that the child cannot be understood (as the child is not 'reasonable'). The parent focuses on the child's behaviour, rather than trying to understand the child's feelings. The belief that the child is unreasonable may arouse anger in the parent, as it can be very frustrating to feel that you are dealing with someone 'unreasonable'. Parents are likely to punish or dismiss the child in such a case and not to meet the child's emotional needs: parents who feel their child is acting unreasonably are likely to lack the motivation to comfort them or help them solve a problem. The parent may believe that there would be no problem, if only the child decided to be 'reasonable'.

Let us consider the situation from the child's position. Imagine interacting with people who assume you are not reasonable. It doesn't matter what you say, if they don't like it, they deem that you are 'unreasonable' and that there is no problem apart from your reaction to the situation. This is likely to make a person feel hopeless and angry, and behavioural and emotional distress is likely to escalate.

Conversely, parents who believe their child is reasonable are likely to interpret the child's behaviour with the premise that from the child's point of view, their behaviour or feelings seem justified. The parent tries to understand their child's perspective. The parent is likely to be concerned about their child's distress, and therefore motivated to help their child emotionally (e.g. by providing soothing or reassurance).

3. My child is (not) genuinely feeling the emotions he is showing

This belief interferes with empathy because it blinds parents to their child's emotional state. A child has limited ways in which to show his distress. It can be argued that a child who is crying and screaming is upset. However, parents may not interpret this as distress. Instead they may think he is trying to get attention by pretending to be upset; or he is trying to manipulate his parents for his own ends; or even that he is screaming and crying to get back at his parents. Crying and screaming are hard to miss (however a person interprets their meaning), but children also show emotions by facial expressions, the extent of their quietness, physical movements and so forth. Parents may misinterpret any of these signs and be perplexed by their child's 'misbehaviour'. Without believing that the child really feels the emotions he is showing, it is not possible for parents to empathise. If parents don't empathise they won't be concerned about the child's distress (the distress won't seem real) and parents are likely to respond by punishing or being dismissive. This leaves the child without support and so his emotions and behaviour tend to escalate (e.g. louder screaming, more severe tantrums).

On the other hand, parents who believe their child is genuinely feeling the emotions he is showing are able to understand their child's emotional state. This allows the parent to put the child's behaviour in the context of his feelings and to empathise with the child's position.

4. My child is (not) emotionally dependent on me

Children are emotionally dependent on their parents and need their parents' support to help them regulate their emotions. Parents who don't believe this are likely to be insensitive in their interactions, and may conclude that there is no need for them to be careful about what they say or do – and so they are more likely to be critical and disparaging of the child, or to act in a way that is hurtful. When children are hurt, they may become withdrawn or even defiant. Withdrawal, defiance, or a blank expression can all serve to convince a parent that the child really does not care about the parent's actions. Sometimes, the more the child is hurt, the less he seems hurt. Children can take a defensive stand and say 'I don't care what you say.' But underneath, children do care – some have lost hope of pleasing their parents, but they are still hurt by criticism or feeling dismissed and not being listened to.

On the other hand, parents who understand the extent to which their child is sensitive to what they say and do are likely to be considerate. This encourages the child to trust the parents and to communicate openly. Children who are hurt by their parents (whether or not the parents are aware of the hurt they are causing) tend to be protective of themselves and to not be open about their feelings.

Flowcharts 1 and 2 (see next page) show this model of empathy. Flowchart 1 shows that positive beliefs about a child will help a parent to empathise. In the case where the parent empathises, the child's emotional needs are likely to be met, so he will feel better (and therefore behave better). The improved behaviour then reinforces the parent's beliefs that the child is reasonable and has a good character. In contrast, when the parent does not empathise, the child's emotional needs are not met, as shown in Flowchart 2. The child is likely to feel ignored or attacked and then to behave in a worse manner. The worse behaviour then reinforces the parent's belief that there is something amiss in the child's character (that he is hostile or unreasonable).

When a parent empathises

Flowchart 1

Megan's beliefs about her daughter Holly
She is a kind person.
She is reasonable.
She really feels the emotions she shows.
She is affected by what I (Megan) say to her.

When Holly has a fight with her sister, Megan thinks Holly must have been upset by something.
She asks Holly what happened.
She thinks about the feelings causing her behaviour.

Megan's reaction
► concern for both daughters
► tells Holly not to be rough with her sister
► listens to Holly's point of view
► helps Holly to calm down.

Effect on Holly
► feels that her mother cares for her, so she recovers from the upset with her sister and is able to be friendly again
► behaves calmly again, which reinforces Megan's positive beliefs.

When a parent does not empathise

Flowchart 2

Bridget's beliefs about her son Terence
He is hostile.
He is unreasonable.
He fakes his feelings to get attention.
He is not affected by what I (Bridget) say to him.

**When Terence has a fight with his brother,
Bridget thinks that he probably started it.**
She doesn't try to find out Terence's point of view.
She focuses on his behaviour, not his feelings.

Bridget's reaction
- feels anger
- yells at Terence
- punishes Terence
- ignores his protests and crying.

Effect on Terence
- upset that his mother won't listen to him
- becomes even more angry
- feels that his mother doesn't care about his side of the story
- behaves more aggressively, which reinforces Bridget's negative beliefs.

WHAT CAUSES NEGATIVE OR POSITIVE BELIEFS ABOUT YOUR CHILD?

There is a range of factors that may contribute to you forming beliefs about your child.

Beliefs and expectations held prior to the child's birth

Even before your baby is born, you start to form ideas and expectations of what your child will be like. These can be positive (e.g. a belief that the baby is a good human being deserving of care) or negative (e.g. a belief that the baby will be difficult). These initial beliefs can affect how you respond to your child in his early days of life, which may then affect how the child develops.

Consider this scenario: a mother believes that her unborn child will be difficult and demanding (this is her experience of her relationship with the baby's father). When the child is born, he cries (naturally enough) and is not able to be soothed straight away in the first few weeks of life. She interprets this as evidence that the baby is 'difficult' and she grows to resent this aspect of the baby's behaviour. This interferes with her care giving as she is not as motivated to soothe her child. As the child doesn't receive the comfort he requires, he is likely to cry more. And so a pattern is established, which was contributed to by the mother's initial beliefs. Of course the mother's beliefs are only part of the story because if the child had been born with a placid temperament, her initial belief may have vaporised.

The child's crying, however, may be interpreted differently. A mother who believed prior to the child's birth that her baby deserved care and was special may interpret the child's crying differently. The crying may be seen as evidence that her child needs extra help to adjust to the world and so her responsiveness may have increased, resulting in the baby having his emotional needs met.

A resemblance to a liked/disliked relative

A child may resemble a relative whom the parent particularly likes or dislikes. The resemblance may be physical (he has his grandfather's eyes), or it may be a personality trait ('he is fussy and pedantic like my aunt'). The parent then believes that the child not only shares a specific physical or behavioural trait, but also resembles the person more fully in their personality. This can easily become what is known as a 'self-fulfilling prophecy'. For example, Gino has his grandfather's eyes. Because of this striking similarity, his parents also conclude that Gino is kind and thoughtful like his grandfather. This belief influences how the parents interpret Gino's actions. Every time he does something thoughtful and kind, they comment on it and tell him how considerate he is. Times when he is not thoughtful are seen as an aberration, not a reflection of Gino's 'true' character. Gino does become kind and thoughtful because he is told he is that kind of a person so regularly that he comes to believe it.

On the other hand, parents may believe that a child has the manipulative streak of his grandmother. When the child is being 'difficult', the parents nod their head knowingly – this is his 'true' character. Such a belief can interfere with parents trying to understand what the child is feeling and thinking because they assume that they know what is fuelling the behaviour (the manipulative streak).

Stress or adverse events

When parents feel overwhelmed by life's circumstances they may have less psychological energy to devote to trying to understand their child. A lack of understanding can impair their emotional care of the child. The child may react to the lack of emotional care he is receiving by behaving in a way that shows his distress. Then the child's emotional or behavioural problems reinforce the parents' negative views about the child.

Parents who received poor parental care themselves

Parents who received parental care that did not meet their emotional needs are more prone to having difficulties with parenting. This is by no means inevitable. It may be, however, that in such cases parents are more likely to develop negative beliefs about their children (possibly their own parents had negative beliefs about them), which may resurface in a parent's mind when they observe their own child's behaviour and influence their interpretations and behaviours toward their child.

The child's behaviour

Children vary in their temperament, their activity level, sociability and so on. Children vary in the speed with which they develop. Some four-year-olds can concentrate for long periods of time; others are distractible and need lots of external structure to help them accomplish tasks. If a child is exhibiting behaviour that is disruptive, challenging or just time-consuming, then it is easier to conclude that maybe he does have a bad character; maybe he is hostile and manipulative (why else would he ask me for more lollies ten times in a row?). The child's actual behaviour can influence parents' beliefs about their child. The challenge is to help the child to improve his behaviour and to develop in a healthy manner, without developing negative beliefs about him. Negative beliefs will interfere with your ability to meet your child's emotional needs, which in turn, will impact on his development and wellbeing.

Evaluations of the child by relatives and friends

It is not only parents who evaluate a child's behaviour; extended family, friends and members of the community may all have an opinion about the child's development and behaviour. This is especially likely for children who have behaviour that is harder to manage – maybe the child cries easily, is hard to settle, or very active. Relatives and friends can have a significant impact on your beliefs about your child. You may try to be positive, making allowances for your child, maybe trying to understand what is happening for him. Relatives and friends, however, may be critical and insinuate that your child is spoilt or trying to control you, or just putting on a performance for some attention. Or they may tell you that their child had similar issues and grew out of them. You may feel relieved it's a developmental stage, rather than reflecting a problem with your child.

EMPATHY AND YOUR CHILD'S BEHAVIOUR

All children, at times, behave in ways that are socially inappropriate, disruptive or otherwise unacceptable to the parents. Being empathic does not mean that you let your child do whatever he wants to. A large part of parenting is teaching your child how to adapt and how to behave in ways that are socially acceptable. Empathising with your child gives you the best chance to help your child behave because you are aware of his perspective. You are open to what might be causing his behaviour. In some cases your child misbehaves because he is feeling hurt or angry; at other times he is overexcited; at other times he is bored; and yet still other times he may have seen this behaviour on television or in the playground, and is trying it out (e.g. giving someone a karate chop). In such cases, you are faced with behaviour that needs a response. The strategies you use to help your child behave will be different depending on the reasons underlying the behaviour. If your child is misbehaving because of boredom, it makes sense to provide activities or structure his time. If he is imitating undesirable behaviour seen on television, then reducing exposure to violent shows (or shows depicting poor manners) is a good idea. If your child is too young to behave appropriately in certain contexts (e.g. a toddler unable to sit through a show), provide alternative activities for him.

MISBEHAVIOUR VERSUS CHILDREN'S DISTRESS

It is not uncommon for children to behave in socially unacceptable ways when they are feeling upset or angry. At such times, children need help managing their emotions. For example, if your child is angry (even over something trivial), he needs someone to listen to him, someone to take him seriously and to help him calm down. When distress and misbehaviour occur together, ideally you should consider your child's feelings as well as his behaviour. You need to make it clear what behaviour is acceptable, but also soothe your child if he is distressed.

Responding to undesirable behaviour

While it may be difficult to remain calm when faced with your child's undesirable behaviour, it is important that you do so to try to help him change his behaviour.

Outline the inappropriate behaviour

Clearly state what it is about the behaviour you don't approve of and what behaviour is more appropriate. If your child snatches from his sibling, you might say 'Please don't snatch, wait your turn and say please.' A child who hits a sibling might be told 'Don't hit your sister, speak to her about what is upsetting you or come and tell me so I can help you sort it out.'

Address the issue that is fuelling the behaviour

When parents empathise with their child, they are likely to think about what is underlying the child's behaviour. For example, an aggressive child may be retaliating because of teasing by siblings. Addressing the teasing is as important as explaining to the child she shouldn't hit or swear. A child who is bored needs to be redirected or provided with suggestions for activities. If your child says 'There's nothing to do', you might suggest three or four activities that he can choose from. If your child is upset, he needs to be soothed. You may be preoccupied with reprimanding your child for his behaviour and forget about his feelings, or think that it is not your place to soothe the child (that he should be able to do it himself). By only reprimanding him, you are only dealing with half the equation – the behavioural half and ignoring the emotional side. When your child has misbehaved you might be angry and this can prevent you from being able to soothe your child. (Children know when someone is annoyed or angry with them, they can see it in the person's facial expression, tone of voice, and so on.)

Help your child to consider the effects of his actions

You need to help your child to consider the effects of his actions on other people. If your child is criticised harshly, denigrated or humiliated, he is likely to feel overwhelmed with guilt or other negative feelings and to stop listening. Adults are the same; we don't like to be harangued. The most common reason that parents lecture is probably because they are not sure that their child is listening to them, so they keep talking! However, in this case, less is more. Clearly and calmly stating your expectations, or the effects of your child's behaviour on others, is likely to be more effective than lecturing. When children feel guilty or ashamed they are unlikely to show their emotions when a parent is explaining the effects of their actions, but it is likely that they are listening.

Your child needs to receive information about how his behaviour is affecting others without being sent on a guilt trip. For example, it is not a good idea to say 'You are making my depression worse and you are ruining my day.' You might say something like 'It hurts your sister's feelings when you call her names. I expect you not to do that again' or, 'When you play so loudly I can't concentrate on my show.' Such communication helps your child to learn to consider other people's needs. This needs to go both ways. If your child feels upset because someone has gone through his toys without asking, or is interfering with him in some way, then you also need to stand up for your child's rights and communicate to the child that his feelings and needs matter as well.

Variability in empathy

Your level of empathy for your child can change depending on the situation you are dealing with and, also, it can change depending on which of your children you are interacting with.

Variability for the same child

Each interaction between you and your child is an opportunity for you to empathise with your child. It would be fair to say that nobody empathises all the time. If you are tired, distracted or preoccupied with something, you are probably less likely to empathise. So there will be variability in the level of empathy that you have for one child in different situations. Variability in your empathy for your child across time might also be influenced by the emotion that your child is feeling. Some emotions may be easier to empathise with (e.g. you may find it easier to empathise when your child is sad than when he is angry). Other parents may find it easier to empathise when their child is feeling happy about an achievement (winning the student of the week award) than when he is worried or insecure. It is possible to empathise with the whole range of emotions that your child experiences, but with some emotions, you might need to make a conscious effort if you want to empathise.

Variability for different children in the same family

There can also be variability in your level of empathy for different children in your family. It can be that you tend to empathise more with one child than another. Such a difference might be caused by:

★ different beliefs about your children

★ different interpretations of behaviour depending on which child is acting in a particular way.

Parents can have different beliefs about different children, and this affects whether they empathise and how they interpret what is going on for their child. For example, Mary's father believes that Mary is a reasonable child who is genuine in her feelings, a good person and emotionally dependent on him. When Mary cries, her father assumes something must be upsetting her. If he cannot find a reason, he concludes that she must have had a hard day and is feeling sensitive. Either way, he tries to help her feel better by helping her problem-solve (if a problem can be identified) or by soothing her. Because he believes that Mary is emotionally dependent on him, he tries to be sensitive in his interactions with her.

In contrast, Mary's father has a less rosy picture of his son Mark. He suspects that Mark has a hostile streak in him, that he tends to be unreasonable, pretends to be upset just to get attention and is not emotionally dependent on him (he suspects that Mark does not pay much attention to what he says and does). If Mark cries, his father is likely to think that he is exaggerating his feelings, or pretending to be upset just to get attention, so the father responds by telling him to cut it out, rather than trying to soothe him. His belief that Mark does not depend on him emotionally affects his reactions to Mark. While he is careful how he responds to Mary to avoid hurting her feelings, he is not worried how he speaks to Mark because he believes Mark doesn't care anyway. Mark's behaviour fuels this perception. When Mark is told off he glares defiantly and says 'I don't care', or looks like he is not even listening. But underneath it, Mark is sensitive and is hurt by his abrasive manner.

Children are sensitive to their parents and sometimes the more they are hurt, the more they try to act as though they don't care. This can be a cover to protect themselves. Your child is hurt by fights they have with you (even if they are the ones who seem to cause the fights). Your child is sensitive to criticism. Of course, this doesn't mean that you shouldn't correct or chastise your child. Indeed, you need to in order to socialise your child in terms of what is acceptable behaviour. But often, less is more. If you clearly state what the problem is, it will often be enough to get your message across. The more you labour the point, the more defensive your child may become.

Benefits of empathy

Empathy is necessary for a positive, rewarding parent–child relationship. Empathy is important for you to:

★ meet your child's emotional needs

★ have a close and positive relationship with your child.

Consequences of lacking empathy

★ a feeling you don't know your child

★ not knowing the best way to respond to your child

★ suspecting your child has emotional needs but not knowing how to meet them

★ finding it hard to 'connect' with your child

★ a feeling that you are not getting through to your child.

INCREASING YOUR EMPATHY

When you empathise with your child, and engage in genuine efforts to soothe and comfort him, your child feels looked after, valued, safe and respected.

Most parents would probably seek to increase their empathy for their child. Here are some steps that may be beneficial.

1. Become aware of your beliefs about your child. If they are negative, challenge them.

2. Cultivate positive beliefs about your child.

3. Try to pause in circumstances where you would normally jump to conclusions and ask yourself: 'What is happening from my child's perspective? If I were crying like that, how would I be feeling?'

4. Notice how your child responds to genuine empathy. You may notice your child calms down more quickly or resumes appropriate behaviour. You are likely to find that your child is more trusting and that you feel more confident.

Summary

▶ Empathy is necessary for you to meet your child's emotional needs.

▶ Your beliefs about your child influence your level of empathy.

▶ The extent to which you empathise will influence your responses to your child.

PART TWO

MEETING YOUR CHILD'S EMOTIONAL NEEDS

The *first* year

L ooking after a baby is intensive work. Because of their immature state, babies are almost entirely dependent on their carers. Babies need a high level of physical and emotional care to develop healthily.

Essentially, babies have two main emotional needs:

1. to be helped with emotional regulation (e.g. soothing when upset)

2. to establish a secure attachment relationship.

These two needs are related; babies who receive help with their emotions also tend to develop secure attachment. One of your baby's major tasks is to learn to trust that her caregivers will care for her, and that the world is a safe and predictable place. Trust comes from experiences of sensitive and consistent care that meets your baby's physical and emotional needs.

Meeting your baby's physical needs is only half the story. Babies have as many emotional needs as they have physical needs.

Babies' physical needs	Babies' emotional needs
Adequate food	Soothing when upset
Physical comfort	Affection
Comfortable temperature	Parents to show interest and happiness when interacting with them
Adequate sleep	Company
Cleanliness	Positive words
Peaceful environment (e.g. not too much noise)	Playful interactions

HELP WITH EMOTIONAL REGULATION

Babies tend to cry easily and frequently. They cry if they are hungry, tired, uncomfortable or lonely. Babies cry easily because they are not able to regulate their emotions as efficiently as adults. When a baby gets upset, she finds it hard to calm down. Your baby is highly dependent on you (or other caregivers) to help her regulate her emotions – it is not something she can do on her own. Babies who are soothed by others better learn how to soothe themselves. This learning process takes place over years, so emotional regulation develops slowly throughout childhood. Developing emotional regulation skills does not mean that children become totally independent, but rather that they have a range of strategies to calm themselves. One strategy for regulating emotions is to seek comfort from others. Even adults, when faced with exciting or distressing news, seek to share that information with the people they are close to, or may need comfort and support. Part of helping your baby regulate her emotions is teaching her that it is okay to receive help and to rely on others.

Risks of not receiving help with emotional regulation

Babies who do not receive help with emotional regulation are at risk of:
- ★ crying for prolonged periods of time
- ★ experiencing less happiness
- ★ compromised emotional development
- ★ taking longer to learn how to regulate their emotions
- ★ experiencing more anger
- ★ having less trust in their caregivers
- ★ insecure attachment.

EMOTIONAL NEEDS MAY BE INCONVENIENT

Your baby's emotional needs may well be inconvenient. You might be busy or tired. Parents do not have endless time for sole attention to one baby. You might have other children to attend to, housework to finish, you might have to get ready for work, and you might want some time to yourself (which is necessary for your own needs to be met). Flexibility and creativity in these situations can be helpful. Can a sibling amuse the baby? A drive in the car might provide everyone in the family with a much needed change of scenery. Your toddler and your baby who is grizzly might welcome a walk in the park.

You might recall the scenario involving Jemima and Barry from Chapter 1 in which Jemima had been teary all day and Barry was having trouble getting her to settle. He was concerned that he may have spoilt Jemima by giving her too much attention.

Jemima's behaviour is normal for a baby in her first year of life. She becomes upset easily, and it is not always about having enough food or sleep. Her emotional needs are for company, feeling secure and interacting with her parents. It is not clear to her father why she has been teary this particular day. Sometimes it is impossible to know for sure what is upsetting a baby. Maybe Jemima is feeling insecure or off colour. Barry need not be concerned about having given his daughter too much attention and responding to her in the past. Attentive parenting does not spoil children, but rather it helps to strengthen them emotionally. Jemima is still very immature emotionally, and while it is frustrating for her dad not to know what is disturbing her, it can be seen from her behaviour that she needs extra emotional care today.

HOW TO MEET YOUR BABY'S EMOTIONAL REGULATION NEEDS

While it takes a lot of effort to meet your baby's emotional regulation needs, it certainly pays off for you and your child in the long run. Babies who are helped to regulate their emotions end up crying less and are more easily soothed than children who are left unattended. A baby who has her emotional needs met is generally easier to look after.

Here are three steps to meeting babies' emotional regulation needs:

Listen to your baby

To help your baby with her emotional needs, it is important to be guided by what she needs at a particular time. Emotional needs need to be met when they arise. An analogy can be made with hydration. Babies need an ongoing supply of liquid to prevent dehydration. It is not possible to meet their need for liquid in one go at a time convenient to you – and so it is with meeting emotional needs.

Listening to your baby will allow you to get information about what your baby needs and how she is feeling. Your baby is the most important source of information about what she needs. You might think your baby shouldn't be upset because you have fed and changed her and provided her with some colourful toys to play with. But if your baby cries when you put her down, then it means something is wrong from her perspective and she needs your help to feel better. Any number of solutions may be appropriate. A parent who has some free time might hold the baby for a while or place the baby near where they are doing a chore. Yet other solutions might be to put on some music or give her another set of toys that might take her interest.

Try to empathise with your baby

For parents to help their babies with emotional regulation, they need to empathise. Empathy is important for these reasons:

Understanding what your baby is experiencing

When you empathise with your baby you are putting yourself in her shoes. What would it feel like to be a baby lying in a cot feeling uncomfortable? When you understand your baby's experience, you are much more able to help her. If you think your baby is lonely, you might provide company; if she is scared, you could reassure her. When parents empathise with their baby, they are taking the baby's feelings seriously.

Motivation to help your baby

When you empathise with your baby it generally motivates you to help her. Your baby needs your help frequently, so staying motivated is important for providing good quality care. When you really believe that your baby is suffering (e.g. feeling sad, lonely or uncomfortable) and not just crying for the sake of it, you are more likely to find the energy to help her yet again.

Communicating empathy to your baby

Interacting with your family and friends, you sense when someone truly understands you. They say and do things that show you that they care. You might recognise that the person empathises with you by their tone of voice, a look, a hug, or a reassuring word. On the other hand, when someone misses the point of what you are trying to communicate, their response jars with you. You are likely to feel annoyed rather than comforted by the person's response. If you understand what your baby is feeling, you are more likely to be able to be effective in soothing her.

Feeling less resentful about the baby's demands

If you empathise with your baby you are likely to see her crying (or other behaviour) as stemming from a genuine need, rather than thinking that she is just being annoying or making unreasonable demands. You are likely to feel less annoyed, and to be more concerned for your baby's wellbeing (rather than being preoccupied with your own irritation).

Respond to your baby

Once you have listened to your baby and tried to empathise, the next step is to respond. This may involve talking to your baby (even young babies may be soothed by your voice), picking her up, rocking her, singing to her, and so on. The response you make depends not only on what your baby is signalling (crying versus cooing), but also on where you are and what you are doing. If you can't get to your baby straight away because you are in the middle of something, you might speak to her (or sing to her!). When you empathise with your baby, you are more likely to be calm and to be able to respond in a way that is helpful for your baby such as speaking soothingly, handling her gently, and so on.

Peta is a 25-year-old who had a baby earlier in the year. While she had been looking forward to the birth of her first child, she found the first few months frustrating. She was surprised that Zac needed her most of the time. Her mother had warned her about not 'spoiling' him and told her that if she gave him attention every time he cried, he would become impossible to look after. So when she fed and changed Zac and he still cried, Peta would ignore him. She thought he needed to learn to be independent – but he just cried and cried (eventually he would fall asleep). Then she read something about children's emotional needs and she realised that Zac needed her care and company as much as he needed food and sleep. She tried to be more attentive to him, and when he cried, she thought about how much he was depending on her, rather than thinking he needed to learn to cope by himself. When he started to cry, she would pick him up. Within a week or so, she found that he was settling more quickly because he knew she would be trying to comfort him. He became more responsive – sometimes he would stop crying as soon as he heard her voice saying 'Here I am, Zac, everything's fine.' Meeting Zac's emotional needs did take a lot of time – although she no longer saw it as a nuisance, but rather as important as feeding and changing him. She enjoyed being a mother more once she let herself meet Zac's emotional needs.

HELPING YOUR BABY ESTABLISH A SECURE ATTACHMENT RELATIONSHIP

Babies need to feel emotionally secure and to develop trust in their caregivers. Babies are social beings – their wellbeing depends significantly on the quality of their relationships with their parents/caregivers. You are much more likely to enjoy a healthy emotional relationship with your baby if you are able to help her develop a secure attachment to you. A secure attachment relationship sets the stage for the baby to be able to reveal her feelings and communicate openly as she develops language.

What does it mean for a baby to feel secure?

The baby is confident that her parent will help her when she needs help. It is pretty bleak if we think that people will only want to be with us in good times. Ideally a sense of security is established in the first year of life. However, it is never too late to try to increase your baby's feelings of security.

Promoting secure attachment in your baby

Parents who respond to their baby's distress sensitively and supportively, and who are warm and consistent in their care, are helping their baby to develop trust in them and to develop a secure attachment to them. In terms of responding to your baby's distress, the key is to intervene as soon as possible. If you wait till your baby is screeching, it is far more difficult to soothe her.

Positive face-to-face interactions with caregivers

Synchronous interactions are important. These are interactions that are 'in tune' so that the parent reacts a certain way depending on what the baby is doing. Verbal give and take, where both you and your baby have a turn at communicating helps your baby to develop emotionally. Positive and warm interactions are nurturing for your baby, and they increase your baby's sense of security.

Respond sensitively

Being sensitive means that that you take cues from your baby. You consider what she is feeling and experiencing and make a response in relation to that. For example, your baby is crying, and so you pick her up.

Be guided by your baby's responses

Imagine this: your baby is crying and you think your baby is hungry so you offer her milk. The baby turns her head away. At this point you might make two interpretations:

1. My baby is being difficult and refusing to feed. I will let her cry.

2. My baby isn't hungry (or is frustrated by a slow flow of milk, or there is insufficient milk, or teething is causing pain). I'll try some other way to comfort her.

By remaining open to your baby's reactions to your efforts, you are focused on trying to help your baby and are prepared to try a range of things, rather than giving up prematurely if she continues to cry.

Be consistent in attending to your baby's distress

There is a myth that attending to a baby's cries spoils the baby. The evidence, however, is clear that the more consistently you respond to your baby's distress, the less your baby cries. One of the building blocks of emotional security is consistency of care. For your baby to establish a secure attachment relationship, she needs to trust that you will be there for her when she needs you. Trust is built on actual experiences.

Warm and happy interactions

Observations of parents and babies have shown that babies are strongly influenced by their parents' facial expressions and tone of voice. Parents who smile and show warmth have a much greater chance of the baby responding positively than parents who are blank or negative in their expression. Babies need happy and warm interactions with their parents and caregivers.

Won't I spoil my baby?

No. Babies are not spoilt by having their emotional needs met. Meeting your baby's emotional needs is a fundamental and important thing that you can do to help her have emotional and mental health in the present and future. When a baby has a secure attachment she knows that she can gain help when she needs it. By insisting your baby manage her own emotions before she is ready to is likely to delay rather than progress her emotional development and her ability to manage her emotions.

Nadia is an eight-month-old girl who loves spending time with her father, Jack. Jack felt some uncertainty about becoming a parent when Nadia was born, but he wanted to develop a close relationship with his daughter and he knew that he had to make time for her. In the first few months of her life, he made sure he spoke warmly to her, sang a couple of nursery rhymes he knew, and gave her her evening bath. When she cried, he consoled her, and he felt a deep satisfaction that he could make her feel better. Now that she is a bit older, she laughs at his antics, smiles enthusiastically when he comes home from work, and he saw her crawl for the first time when they were playing a peek-a-boo game. Jack can see how his efforts to communicate and care for his daughter have paid off, and he looks forward to keeping a close relationship going as she grows.

The risks of not establishing a secure attachment

Babies who are insecurely attached are anxious about whether their needs will be met. Some babies withdraw and learn to keep their feelings to themselves because they know that they will not receive help when they need it (avoidant attachment). Other babies became clingy and cry inconsolably, even if someone is trying to soothe them (anxious attachment). Insecure attachment is related to the baby finding it hard to trust others and often these children develop a negative image of themselves as unlovable and unworthy of care.

Be wary of pitfalls such as detachment and intrusiveness.

Detachment

Babies, like adults, need involvement with other people. They need someone looking out for their wellbeing (especially because there is so little they can do themselves) and they need to be in a positive relationship with their parents (or caregivers). You may feel detached from your baby because of stress, depression or other difficulties in your life. Sometimes there is no obvious reason, but you have difficulties developing feelings of closeness with your baby. Feelings of detachment are likely to impair the quality of care provided – for example, a parent may not initiate interactions with their baby, or the parent may ignore the baby for prolonged periods of time.

Intrusiveness

We all need personal space, time to collect our thoughts, and rest from interacting with people. As adults we achieve these needs by removing ourselves from other people, by terminating conversations we feel are intrusive, and having some time just to ourselves. Your baby also needs personal space. But she can only have it if her caregivers are sensitive to this need and provide it for her. Your baby can't go for a walk to get away from it all. Your baby can't even move to another room. Babies show they need personal space by eye and body movements. Babies may look away when they feel over-stimulated, or when they don't want to interact, or they may arch or move their bodies to show they need some space. Intrusiveness occurs when caregivers miss a baby's signals that she needs space and time to herself and continue to interact with the baby or force eye contact. You can avoid intrusiveness by listening to your baby's verbal and nonverbal signals that she needs quiet time.

YOUR BELIEFS

Your beliefs about your baby influence how you feel about her, and have a big impact on the way you respond (or don't respond). In the course of our everyday lives we don't often take time to examine what we are thinking, or how we are interpreting a situation. When we are aware of our thoughts, we tend to consider them reflections of reality rather than ideas that might be biased and need challenging. Parents are likely to think that the beliefs they have about their baby are accurate.

Positive beliefs and interpretations will help parents to have the motivation and persistence required to meet their baby's emotional needs. Negative beliefs compromise parents' ability to meet their baby's emotional needs.

Helpful beliefs

We have seen that there are particular beliefs that will help parents to empathise and meet their baby's needs. Let's look at the beliefs that will specifically help parents of babies.

My baby has a good character

Even at this early stage in a baby's life, parents may believe their baby has a good or bad character. If you believe your baby has a good character, you are motivated to care for her and to be responsive. You may feel you can trust your baby so when she cries, you believe she really is upset and needs help rather than thinking she is inherently 'difficult'. In contrast, if you suspect your baby has a bad character, you are likely to feel manipulated and are less likely to respond when your baby is upset.

My baby is reasonable

If you believe that your baby is reasonable, you will assume there must be a real reason for her to be crying. Maybe your baby is in pain, uncomfortable, or something else is upsetting her. The assumption is that your baby's reactions genuinely stem from her experiences. This makes you believe that it is possible to understand her, even if you don't know exactly what is wrong. If your baby is crying, you know something is wrong from her perspective.

My baby really feels the emotions she shows

Parents who see their baby's displays of emotion as genuine can respond appropriately to what their baby needs. When your baby smiles or laughs, she is happy and you join in. A moment later your baby starts crying, indicating that something has upset her. You don't need to second-guess your baby; you can take her communication of her emotions at face value.

My baby depends on me emotionally and is affected by our interactions

Parents who understand the extent to which their baby depends on them emotionally are more mindful of how they interact with their baby. The parent can appreciate how much it means to the baby when the parent smiles and gives the baby a hug, or sings a nursery rhyme or pats her when she is crying.

Unhelpful beliefs

Holding negative beliefs about your baby is likely to hinder your ability to support her emotionally.

My baby is manipulative/has a bad character

Parents are not going to want to attend to their baby if they believe that she is manipulating them. Some parents find it hard to attend to their crying baby consistently. They may feel that the baby is trying to control them or that they are spoiling their baby. A parent may alternate between attending to their baby and feeling manipulated and not attending to the baby. This is confusing for the baby and of course, the times when the baby is not being attended to, the baby is likely to cry. Parents may interpret this as meaning that they have given the baby too much attention but it is normal for babies to require a lot of soothing and interaction because of their emotional immaturity.

My baby is unreasonable

You may have fed and changed your baby, but she is still crying. If you think that your baby is being 'demanding' and 'unreasonable' you are likely to stop trying to make her feel better. It can set up a battle instead of a cooperative relationship.

My baby is whingeing for no good reason

Interpreting your baby's crying as not really indicating distress (as least not the same level of distress that would be experienced by an adult crying the same way) reduces your motivation to attend to your baby.

My baby is not emotionally dependent on me

This devalues the contribution and the central role you have in your baby's life. It is hurtful for you to feel that you don't matter the way you should. You may feel this way if you are experiencing difficulties, if others are undermining your parenting, or if you lack confidence in the parenting role. You may feel that no matter what you do, you are not really having an impact on your baby's development.

Here are some other beliefs that can interfere with your empathy for your baby, and so reduce the emotional care you provide:

★ It doesn't hurt my baby to cry.

★ Crying is good exercise for the lungs.

★ Babies need to know that they don't always get what they want.

★ Babies who are often attended to get spoilt.

These beliefs will encourage you not to attend to your baby. A baby whose emotional needs are not adequately met will tend to cry more, or become withdrawn and uncommunicative. Either way, your baby is likely to be more difficult to look after, both in the present and the future. This puts further stress on you when you are probably already feeling overwhelmed. Once habits are established, they have a tendency to persist. However, if you make a conscious effort to examine what is going on and try to alter your thoughts and behaviours, there is potential to turn things around.

Most parents have negative thoughts about their baby at some time or another. This is a natural part of the stress of parenting. It is important to be aware of your thoughts and interpretations about your baby. When you are aware of your negative thoughts, you can challenge them and try to replace them with more positive thoughts that make it easier for you to give your baby good quality care.

Positive interpretations of a baby's crying

★ She needs me because I am her mum/dad.

★ She is lonely and needs company.

★ She is uncomfortable.

★ She is sad.

★ She is too young to calm herself; she needs my help.

Negative interpretations of a baby's crying

★ She is spoilt.

★ She is just crying to get attention and if I give it to her, she will want more.

★ She is never satisfied with the care I provide.

★ She has to learn to sort herself out otherwise I'm making a rod for my own back.

★ It doesn't matter if my baby cries; it doesn't do her any harm.

Such interpretations will not motivate you to attend to your baby. Research has shown that babies who are attended to quickly and consistently cry less than babies who are not.

TEMPERAMENT

Babies have different temperaments. Some sleep well, feed well and are generally content with minimal care, and it seems the parent doesn't have to do much to satisfy the baby. Other babies wake frequently, cry easily and for prolonged periods of time, and have feeding difficulties.

It is not known to what extent temperament is biologically determined, and to what extent the environment shapes the baby's temperament. It is generally believed that temperament is biologically based but that it is modified by the experiences the child has in their daily life.

These issues aside, it is known that babies do differ in the way they behave and interact with the world. It is easier to care for a baby who has an easy temperament. Parents of babies with more difficult temperaments face a number of challenges. A key challenge is to provide high quality care despite your baby's temperament. It can be hard to maintain positive views and interpretations of your baby (especially if people label her as 'difficult' or are concerned that she is so 'demanding'). In fact you may be blamed for being too indulgent. The challenge is to accept your baby's temperament as something out of your baby's control, but something that impacts on your baby's wellbeing. It's a bit like having sensitive teeth. No-one chooses to have sensitive teeth, but the fact they do means that cold food may hurt them.

The danger is that parents may somehow blame the baby for her temperament. Of course no-one would do this consciously, but it can be hard to separate a baby from her temperament. During the early months, we are in the process of getting to know our baby, and in that process we form opinions. If the baby is crying and fussing a lot, it can be hard to see past that. If the baby is blamed for her temperament, or if parents don't keep attending to the baby with empathy and soothing, there is the risk that the baby's crying and fussing will worsen, or at the least, not decline. One study found that parents of babies who were classed as having a difficult temperament ended up securely attached if the parents received support so that they continued to be responsive to their babies.

SLEEP (OR LACK THEREOF)

One of the most vexing issues in the baby's first year of life is sleep (or to be more precise, a lack of sleep). Sleeping can seem problematic if your baby is waking frequently or taking a long time to settle at night. With many parents working, it has become a pressing issue. If you have to go to work the next day, sleep deprivation can impact on you dramatically. Many parents now don't have the luxury of catching up on sleep during the day when the baby sleeps.

Your baby's sleep cycles are different from childhood and adult patterns and many babies don't sleep through the night for some time. Then there is the pain associated with teething, or having a longer nap in the car might mean the baby is not tired at her usual bedtime. Unlike an older child who might amuse herself or read (or lie in bed quietly for a while), a baby in her first year of life is not likely to have the reasoning skills to cope with that. So your baby might cry and fuss if left in the cot. There is also the issue of separation anxiety and loneliness. Your baby may want company and feel insecure if left by herself. Sure, you know there's nothing to worry about – your baby has received food, and is warm, and everyone is home. But your baby does not have the same reasoning skills. All she is experiencing is the feeling of being left alone. This is upsetting and so your baby cries.

Getting a reasonable amount of sleep need not conflict with meeting your baby's emotional needs. Your baby's emotional needs don't switch off when the sun goes down. Some ways that your baby's sleeping habits can be improved are:

1. *A soothing bedtime routine.* Sometimes the difficulty in getting to sleep is due to over-stimulation and the baby doesn't know how to calm herself. Limiting the amount of stimulation a baby has might help with sleep.

2. *Soothing music or mobile.* Your baby may find the sound of quiet music or the gentle movement of a mobile mesmerising and may be lulled off to sleep.

3. *Staying quietly with the baby until she falls asleep.* If you feel this might be too boring, you could bring a book with you – or you might find that you relax along with your baby.

4. *Sleeping with the baby in your bed.* This should not be done if you are medicated, intoxicated, sleeping on very soft bedding or are overweight, as suffocation may occur.

5. *Having the baby's cot in your room* so that when the baby awakes you don't have to go to another room to attend to her.

You need to feel comfortable with whatever method you choose. Whether or not to practise co-sleeping is a personal choice. Some parents will feel strongly that their baby needs to be in another bed or another room, while others will be equally adamant that their baby needs to be in bed with them. There are many ways to meet your baby's needs, and the individual preferences of parents can be accommodated.

YOUR BABY'S EMOTIONAL NEEDS CAN BE CONSTANT

The demands of meeting your baby's constant emotional needs can be exhausting. The unrelenting nature of the demands can mean that even the most positive parent can end up feeling exasperated. Parents need support, time out, relaxation, their own interests and someone to listen to them.

SHE CAN'T TELL YOU WHAT SHE NEEDS

It would be easier to empathise and meet your baby's needs if she were to tell you what was upsetting her or what she needed. When your baby is crying often, or for prolonged periods of time, it can be tempting to tune out and not consider it genuine communication. It can take effort to imagine what is going on for your baby. How is my baby feeling? What might be upsetting my baby now (especially given I have fed and changed her recently)? Your baby can't speak, so you can only attempt to construct what is going on with limited information.

OTHER PEOPLE'S OPINIONS ABOUT WHAT YOU SHOULD BE DOING

Comments and criticism from others can hurt you, make you doubt yourself and confuse you so that you are preoccupied with fending off suggestions rather than empathising with your baby. Other people might even encourage you not to empathise, saying that you are spoiling your baby or that your baby is too demanding.

YOUR OWN EMOTIONAL NEEDS

Parents have their own emotional needs. If your needs are not being met, it makes it harder (though not impossible) for you to meet your baby's needs. The first year of a baby's life brings huge changes in your emotions and experiences. Some of the emotional needs of parents are:

1. to be listened to and nurtured. This might be met by talks with your partner, a relative or friends.

2. to have some time doing activities you enjoy. This can be refreshing and invigorating. Reading, gardening, playing sport, needlework, catching up on news or going for coffee or a walk can provide some emotional space so that you can recharge your batteries.

FATIGUE AND DEPRESSION

If you are feeling low or depressed then you are likely to find it harder to tune into your baby's needs. Every parent has bad days, but if it is a frequent event, then it is advisable to seek help from your general practitioner or a psychologist. If you are overwhelmed and feel that you cannot cope with parenting the way you would like to, you could talk to:

★ your partner

★ a maternal and child health nurse who might be able to help, or refer you to appropriate services

★ your doctor

★ a psychologist.

You may feel embarrassed about seeking help, but there are many professionals available to you who can help you to feel better and manage your parenting responsibilities more easily.

CHILDCARE IN THE FIRST YEAR

These days, childcare is commonly used in the first year of a child's life. Often, there is trepidation about childcare and whether it is in the child's best interests. From the point of view of the baby's emotional needs, the questions are as follows:

★ Is my baby happy to be there? Children will generally need time to become familiar with the staff and surroundings before they would be happy to stay.

★ Are my baby's emotional needs going to be met? What is the caregiver's ability and attitude to responding to children's distress? Some caregivers have more children than they can respond to in a reasonable amount of time, so that despite their best efforts, children are left to cry. Some caregivers don't consider it necessary to respond to crying. Look for carers who are warm and nurturing, and take seriously the emotional needs of the children in their care.

★ Are the caregivers consistent? Children need to be cared for by a consistent group of caregivers. To be left with different people can be frightening and confusing.

Physical surroundings, adequate food and provision of toys are often looked at when quality of childcare is examined. In some ways, the physical surroundings are easier to judge. If the paint is peeling off the walls, or the cots look grubby, parents would be hesitant to leave their child there. Well-resourced centres with colourful toys, big windows and bright mobiles are reassuring. The emotional climate of a place is harder to judge – it may not be evident in the first few minutes. To get an understanding of how children are looked after and responded to, it is a good idea to spend a day or two in the place. What happens when children become distressed? Are they comforted or left to cry? Are the interactions between the staff and children warm and supportive, or tense? These are some indicators of the extent to which the centre is likely to meet your baby's emotional needs.

Summary

▶ Your baby's emotional needs in the first year are constant.

▶ Her two main needs are to form a secure attachment relationship and to receive consistent and prompt help with regulating her emotions.

▶ Babies who have their emotional needs met are in a better position to develop good emotional health in toddlerhood and beyond.

From one to four years

Children between the ages of one and four years experience huge changes in their emotions. Parents may be concerned to see their child transform from a placid baby into a toddler who has tantrums. Children develop rapidly during this time, learning to talk and walk, and gaining a great deal of knowledge about the world.

Emotional changes in the toddler years

The child is likely to experience:

★ an increase in anger and frustration

★ more intense negative emotions

★ tantrums when overwhelmed by negative emotions

★ rapid changes in mood

★ a drive to do things for himself (and anger if his plans are thwarted).

Emotional needs from one to four years

Children in this age group have three main emotional needs:

★ help with regulating their emotions

★ secure attachment

★ to receive understanding about their drive to be independent.

DEALING WITH TANTRUMS

Children between the ages of one and four years need frequent help with regulating their feelings. They can easily become upset and frustrated, and their negative emotions may build up and overwhelm them. Tantrums – a common point of discussion with parents – are visible and often highly audible! They can happen in public places, when you have guests and at many other inconvenient times. Many children go through phases of having tantrums, and they are a normal part of your child's development. There are a number of factors behind your child's tantrums. These include:

★ your child experiencing intense emotions

★ your child having a clearer idea of what he wants to do (as opposed to when he was a baby)

★ your child not having the maturity to deal with his emotions.

However, you need to be concerned about your child's tantrums if:

★ they are severe, for example if your child pulls his hair or physically destroys objects

★ your child has prolonged tantrums (regularly taking more than fifteen minutes to calm down)

★ tantrums are constant throughout the day.

Rethinking tantrums

It is often taken for granted that children throw tantrums for the sake of a performance to try to get what they want. The rationale is that children are calculating how much noise and disturbance they need to make to frazzle their parents enough to give them what they want.

But let us consider another possibility. When children are overwhelmed with negative emotions, they have a tantrum. Children get so upset that they have trouble controlling their behaviour (hence the kicking and throwing themselves on the floor) and they cry inconsolably because they are so desperately unhappy. How upset would an adult have to be to cry so intensely?

If you assume that your child is having a tantrum to try to manipulate you, you are not going to want to soothe your child. In contrast, if you consider your child's emotional state, and see tantrums as the struggles your child is having with regulating his emotions, you will want to help him. This does not mean that your child should be given a doughnut before dinner, or that you buy him a chocolate bar at the checkout. It is possible to maintain rules and boundaries, but also to meet your child's emotional needs. These two things are in no way mutually exclusive.

Children who receive help with regulating their emotions are well placed to emerge from toddlerhood with strong emotional regulation skills, better self-esteem and security in their relationship with their parents. Rather than feeling that they will be left to cope on their own, they will be confident of receiving your help when they need it.

Calming a tantrum

Children need help to calm down because they do not have the maturity to calm themselves. Here are some responses that are likely to help the child to calm down:

★ *Stay calm.* It's important to remain calm, otherwise there will be two upset people instead of one. It is not possible for you to calm your child if you feel upset or angry yourself.

★ *Be kind but firm.* Remember that these two things are not mutually exclusive. You can show your child that you understand he is upset *and* let him know that you do not approve of his behaviour at the same time.

★ *State clearly what needs to happen,* acknowledging your child's distress and helping him to calm down (without trying to reason with him too much).

★ *Talk soothingly* (although too much talking can be unhelpful).

★ *Present alternatives.* You might say 'I know you want the chocolate, but dinner is nearly ready. You can have an apple instead, or a glass of juice. Why don't you help me to set the table?' You are not cutting your child off and expecting him to calm himself, but rather you are showing him that you care about his feelings and are trying to accommodate his wishes (while still sticking to the rule that there is no chocolate before dinner).

★ *Show affection.* For example, your child may find it soothing for you to say 'Come and give me a hug.' If your child is too upset to respond and pushes you away, you can try a bit later on when the intensity of the tantrum has subsided and your child is crying less intensely.

★ *Show understanding.* For example, you might say, 'I know you're hungry, dinner will be ready very soon. Come over here, and I'll show you. See, the pie is nearly baked.'

Ineffective responses to a tantrum

These responses are unlikely to be effective in calming a tantrum and, in fact, are likely to make your child even more upset:

★ yelling

★ criticising your child

★ punishing your child (to be punished is upsetting in itself)

★ trying to reason with your child too much. Children do not have the reasoning capabilities of adults. Parents who try to explain everything to the child, and don't want to move on until the child agrees, will overwhelm the child rather than calming him. There are times the child will be upset, this is an inevitable part of being a toddler. You can help by being kind (trying to calm your child) but firm (still getting on with what needs to happen).

★ words by themselves tend to be an ineffective soothing method when people are experiencing intense emotions. Often a child might be able to understand the logic of what the parent is saying, but in the heat of the moment, he is overwhelmed by his emotions, and therefore he cannot think straight.

There is no on/off switch

Calming your toddler is a process. If your child is screaming, giving him a hug will not stop the screaming straight away. It can be helpful to see how you might engage your child by talking calmly, asking him what the matter is, addressing his concerns or acknowledging his distress, and the reason for it if it is known. Staying with your child emotionally is important. Just saying to your toddler, 'Talk to me when you are not upset' implies that your child's distress is his problem and something he must deal with himself. A healthier message is, 'I care how you feel and I will try to make you feel better.' Again, you are not telling your child that he will get what he wants, but that he will receive support.

Ignoring tantrums

Some people believe that tantrums should be ignored. The difficulty with this approach is that tantrums are a sign of emotional distress indicating that the child needs help with his emotions. None of us like to be ignored when we are upset; in fact, that is quite upsetting in itself. By helping to soothe your child, you are not encouraging tantrums, you are helping your child to calm down.

Preventing tantrums

It is not character building for your child to have tantrums. Some might argue that a child needs to learn that he can't have everything he wants. Certainly, you need to set rules and limits, but your child getting upset does not really help the learning process. If you can see that doing things in a different sequence, or giving something else to your child, or diverting his attention reduces the likelihood of a tantrum, then you are helping your child to regulate his emotions by regulating his environment. It's a bit like putting on the heating so he doesn't have to experience the full brunt of the winter chill. Of course, there will be times when you choose not to change things. For example, if the family is going on an outing but your toddler refuses to leave his playdough, firmly insisting on it and removing the child is fine, but it is also important to try to soothe the child. You could say, 'Would you like to read a book instead' or 'Why don't you help me carry the present for Grandma?' In this case you are getting on with what you need to do, but you are also helping your child cope with the situation emotionally.

RESPONDING TO EMOTIONS

Your responses to your child's emotions have a big impact on his emotional development and his ability to regulate his emotions as he grows. It is important for you to tolerate and accept your child's feelings and respond in a supportive manner. Given the natural increase in your child's negative emotions as he becomes a toddler this can present a challenge.

Broadly speaking, there are three ways you can respond to your child if he is showing negative feelings such as sadness or anger.

Dismissive

Remember that your child looks to you for approval and acceptance. Your words and actions affect them a great deal. By saying things like 'Don't be a sook' or by ignoring your crying child, you may give your child the impression that you are minimising or dismissing your child's emotions.

The messages your child is likely to receive are:

★ 'My mum/dad doesn't care about how I feel.'

★ 'My mum/dad doesn't understand how I feel.'

★ 'My feelings don't matter.'

Punitive

Parents may punish their child for showing negative feelings or threaten the child with punishment if they don't stop. For example, Harry is crying over a broken toy and his mother says 'if you don't stop crying I'll take it away and you won't see it again'. Parents tend to use a punitive approach if they feel that is the only way to stop the child from continuing to cry or complain. In the short term it might work. To avoid the punishment, the child may stop crying and complaining. However, the child's emotions have not been dealt with; the child has just suppressed the emotions, and next time something upsetting happens, the child's reaction is likely to be more severe.

The messages your child is likely to receive are:

★ 'I am bad for being upset.'

★ 'I shouldn't feel what I feel.'

Children who are punished or dismissed when they show negative feelings tend to try to keep their feelings under control. This means that when they are upset they are likely to try to keep a lid on their feelings rather than seeking support. The emotions build up over time and when the child can no longer contain them, they spill over and the child cries, screams or has a tantrum. This outburst can happen in response to a minor provocation because the upset has been building up over a number of incidences. It doesn't just reflect the last upsetting thing that has happened. Because the child's reaction seems over the top, parents are even less likely to empathise and be supportive. Rather they are likely to be focused on the intensity of the child's reaction and to insist the child stop the noise. And so the cycle continues, because once again, the child's feelings have not been addressed.

Supportive

You can respond to your child's distress supportively. When you provide support, you help your child to regain his emotional calm. Here are the steps involved in providing support to your child:

1. *Acknowledge your child's emotion* by saying, for example, 'You're feeling upset about this', without making a judgement about it. Notice that the statement isn't 'I know you are upset, but there is nothing to be upset about.' We can probably all remember a time when we thought we should be happy, but we weren't. Our feelings have a life of their own. Emotional health means that we can acknowledge what we feel and deal with it. Trying to rationalise feelings, or deny feelings that we don't think we should have (or our child should have) leads to tension because the feelings don't disappear. On the other hand, allowing ourselves to feel what we feel can be a relief. So when you acknowledge to your child what they are feeling, and accept it (without moralising, judging or contradicting), you are telling your child that it is okay. This encourages your child to accept his own feelings and to gain a greater awareness of them.

You may ask, 'What if my child is jealous when his sibling has a birthday and gets presents? Surely I shouldn't encourage jealousy?' Acknowledging the feeling is not encouraging it, but rather recognising that it is there. The first step in dealing with any emotion is to recognise it. If you act like your child shouldn't be jealous and start to moralise, your child will probably deny feeling jealous. At this point, no further conversation (at least not a two-way conversation) can occur about how to manage the jealousy, or that jealousy is a normal human emotion. On the other hand, if you acknowledge the jealousy and your child admits it (or at least doesn't deny it), there is a chance to actually address the feeling. You might remind your child that he will have his turn next month when it is his birthday. Remind him that he is still an important part of the celebration and that it is hurtful for his sibling to feel that his brother doesn't share the celebration spirit with him. If your child feels listened to, he is much more likely to participate in this conversation and to take it on board and find it useful. If we feel someone doesn't know (or care) how we feel, we tend to remain preoccupied with our feeling and be unable to engage in conversation or problem-solving.

2. *Listen to your child.* Listen patiently to your child's concerns, then let him know you have heard what he has said by repeating it. This shows you are concerned about his point of view.

3. *Help your child to deal with his emotions.* You can help your child to cope with his emotions and address the situation that is causing the distress (or both). For example, James's bike has a flat tyre and he is upset. His father addresses his emotions supportively; he acknowledges that James is upset

and also helps him deal with the situation. He suggests they take the bike to be fixed and that they go for a ride next week. In the meantime, he suggests they find another fun activity to do this weekend.

The message your child is likely to receive are:

★ 'My mum/dad cares how I feel and wants to help me.'

★ 'Emotions can be handled.'

> *Bianca is a two-year-old who is discovering her will. She is not prepared to accept what she is given as readily as she used to – for example, she sometimes insists on having the special blue cup she received on her birthday. Other times, she doesn't want to go to bed, and sometimes cries when it's bathtime because she wants to keep playing with her tea set. Her father, Andrew, knows that Bianca's more difficult behaviour is part of her development. He thinks about her emotional needs and tries to give her choices when possible. He lets her have the blue cup at meal times, but he does insist on bedtime and bathtime, knowing that she is not old enough to be able to reason about such things. When she gets upset, Andrew is supportive: he tries to soothe Bianca, he gets her bath toys out and tries to make it fun. Bianca soon forgets she didn't want to have a bath. Likewise, at bedtime, he reads to her and gives her cuddles, but does insist that she remain in bed.*

SECURE ATTACHMENT

The same type of parenting that was needed for the establishment of secure attachment during the first year of life is still required. Responsive and sensitive care shows your child in his day-to-day life that he can depend on you when he needs you.

Using you as a secure base

Your child still needs to know that you will be there when he needs help. Your child is now more mobile and so can move away and explore the environment. Being a secure base for your child does not mean you stifle your child's wish for growing independence, but rather support his efforts to try to do things for himself. A parent who is a secure base provides comfort and assistance when the child needs help.

Warm and positive interactions

'Aren't you a sweet boy?' a mother says warmly to her three-year-old child. You can see the glow in his face. He is thrilled that his mother is pleased with him. It is important for him to know that he is approved of, that someone thinks he is wonderful and clever. Of course, there will be times you will not be happy with your child, so it makes it all the more important to seek opportunities to be happy with your child, to praise him, to give him a hug or an encouraging word. It can be easy to forget how dependent your child is on your approval – how much pain it causes when he doesn't receive it and the joy it gives when he does.

Understanding your child's desire for independence

An important part of your child's development during the toddler years is to establish a sense of autonomy and initiative, to establish a sense of his own competencies and wishes. A readjustment needs to occur in the parent–child relationship as a baby becomes a toddler. The parent's role is to encourage the child in his independence while still doing a lot in terms of physical care, organising the day and so on.

Parents can interpret the child coming to them when he needs help in a negative way (they may think it reflects too much dependence). On the other hand, some parents may feel ambivalent about not being needed as much and may feel rejected when the child tries to do everything for himself.

THINGS THAT MAY GO WRONG DURING THE TODDLER YEARS

The toddler years are a challenging time for parents. Here are some things to watch out for.

Expecting your child to manage his own emotions

Parents may assume that a child is more mature than he really is. Children are not able to manage their emotions by themselves. Insisting that your child manage his own emotions, or cutting him off from support (for example, insisting he stay in his room until he is calm) is assuming that he has the skills which should actually be developed in the process of being cared for. Support needs to be offered to a child when he is upset, not just when he is smiling.

Feeling resentful of your child's drive for independence

Toddlers have a drive to do things themselves. This initiative can cause conflict between parents and children. Your child's wishes may differ to yours. He may not want to tidy up, go for a walk or put on his shoes.

When a child discovers his will, the parent may interpret this as the child deciding he is against the parent. This perception may be fuelled by the child insisting on having the cup he wasn't given, and by refusing the parent's help for tasks that not so recently the parent had to do for the child, such as dressing the child. Parents can be disconcerted by this show of will and insistence. Trying to understand your child, and empathising with him as he discovers and asserts his will, is critical for you to continue in a positive relationship with your child. In some cases, the parent has struggled to care for the child as an infant, and toddlerhood brings more woe. In such cases, it may be advisable to seek help in order to prevent establishing a relationship of conflict between yourself and your child, which would cause a lot of heartache for both of you.

Responding in a way that increases your child's distress

You may become angry and upset when your child has a tantrum. This can make you respond in a way that further upsets him rather than calming him.

Struggling to calm your child

You may find it difficult to be able to calm your child. He may spend long periods of time crying and screaming.

Withdrawing support

You may find it difficult to support your child if you can't figure out what he is upset about. Your toddler may be irritable, throw tantrums at the slightest incident and generally seem unhappy. At this point, it is a good idea to ask what is upsetting him. If he tells you what is upsetting him, then you may proceed to be supportive. However, it is common for a child of this age (one to four years) to be unable to specify what the matter is. He either doesn't know why he is unhappy or he doesn't have the words for it. At this point, you may feel like withdrawing support because you cannot get an answer to your queries.

However, even adults can be upset and irritable without knowing the reason. In such situations, adults and children still need support and comfort. In fact, an irritable toddler especially needs help with regulating his emotions. Just because he can't verbalise a reason for his distress doesn't mean that he is not entitled to help with managing his feelings.

Relying on rational explanations

Toddlers can be talkative and seem to understand a lot about the world. This may make parents think that the child is more advanced in his emotional development than he really is. Parents may rely too much on reasoning with their child, and use reasoning to try to calm him, rather than providing emotional support.

Offering emotional soothing and support means:

★ acknowledging your child's feelings without judgement

★ showing you care about how he feels (by what you say and your facial expression)

★ giving your child some time to calm down, rather than expecting an instant response

★ showing affection by giving him a hug or stroking his hair

★ encouraging your child to move to another activity

★ distracting him. You might talk to your child about something he is looking forward to (e.g. 'Remember what we are doing later today?').

Rationalisation means explaining what has to happen and why it has to happen. These explanations should be kept simple and brief otherwise they will further agitate the child, and may encourage him to start arguing.

If you have given your explanation, and your child is still upset, further explanations are unlikely to help. What is more likely to help at this stage is emotional soothing.

YOU ARE A ROLE MODEL

Children learn a lot of skills by observing those around them. This is also true of emotional regulation skills and dealing with emotions. Parents who yell, lose their temper and show aggression when angry may well have children who learn to behave in a similar way. Children can be frightened by parents who don't seem in control of themselves. If you are concerned about the effect your aggression is having on your child, you might consider seeking help for anger management.

CHILDREN DEVELOPING EMPATHY

Children between the ages of one and two years may show empathy for someone who is upset. A child might offer a tissue or give a hug to a person who is crying. Empathy is important for interpersonal relationships. Children who develop empathy for others are likely to cooperate more easily because they understand other people's perspectives. Parents who speak to children about other people's feelings help children to orient themselves towards others' feelings. Discussion of emotions – our own, the child's and other people's – helps the child to develop an understanding of emotion and to see that emotions can be openly dealt with rather than denied. A word of caution is needed here: children who are exposed to the full extent of their parents' negative feelings tend to feel burdened, anxious and will sometimes take a parenting role towards the parent, rather than staying in the role of a child.

The way a child is treated by his parents (and others who care for the child) has a strong influence on the child's development of empathy. Children who are given warm, sensitive care and are shown empathy are more likely show empathy than children who are treated harshly or inconsistently.

EMPATHISING WITH YOUR TODDLER

During toddlerhood your child has to make many adjustments. This period is not easy for your child. He has discovered his will and might often have ideas that he can't clearly communicate. Things that didn't matter a few months ago all of a sudden become an issue (e.g. not wanting to put on shoes, not wanting help with getting dressed, insisting on having a particular cup). These new behaviours can seem arbitrary, and your child's distress when things don't go his way often seems over the top from an adult perspective.

Empathy for your child will help you see the world from your toddler's perspective. This will help you to meet your child's emotional needs and support him through this time of development that can be intense and fraught with emotion.

Benefits of empathising with your toddler

★ developing a close and satisfying relationship

★ knowing what your child's emotional needs are

★ being able to meet your child's emotional needs

★ feeling close to your child rather than feeling you are battling with him.

YOUR NEGATIVE BELIEFS

As discussed previously, there are some negative beliefs you may have about your child that will impact on your empathy for him.

My child is hostile/manipulative

This belief interferes with empathy because the parent assumes that the child's motives are to be oppositional on purpose and to get at the parent. Then the parent feels they are in battle with the child, that there is a power struggle. Battles and power struggles are not conducive to emotional support or meeting your child's emotional needs. Quite the contrary. In such a case the parent will be focused on making sure that the child doesn't win. The outcome is seen in terms of whose will dominates, and there is often distress and anger on both sides in the process. Even when a parent feels they have won, it is a hollow victory, because it is unsatisfying and sad to feel that you are fighting with your child. There can be a sense of estrangement. And soon enough, the battle is on again. If the child gets what he wants, the parent feels they have lost and again the focus is not on what is happening from the child's perspective or what the child needs, but on who is winning.

The child and parent can be on the same side. Both want to get along with each other. Parents want to nurture their children, to have a close and satisfying relationship with them, and to understand their child and help them develop emotionally and socially. Your child needs your support and approval. He can't just switch off all his emotions and his surge for independence, yet he is highly dependent on you for security and for help with his emotions.

If you empathise and see what is happening from your child's point of view, mentally and emotionally, you are in a far better position to stay calm and help him through this time.

A belief that might help you to empathise is 'My child is a good person.' Believing that deep down your child is good means believing that the likely explanation for a tantrum or show of will is not that your child wants to fight with you, but rather that he is attempting to assert his independence. This drive to assert his independence is a natural unfolding of your child's development. It is a normal process of his growth.

My child is unreasonable

This belief doesn't allow parents a chance to try to understand what is going on for the child because they assume there is no logic to what the child is upset about. This belief can short-circuit the empathy process. In contrast, if a parent believes that their child is reasonable and the child is upset or fussing about something that is important to him, the parent tries to consider what might be going on from the child's point of view.

Gus is a boy who has frequent tantrums. Toni, his mother, saw the first evidence of a 'strong will' when he was less than a year old. If he didn't like something, he would scream at the top of his lungs. Now 18 months old, he is having a few tantrums a day. The tantrums last a long time – sometimes he cries for hours. Toni believes that Gus is just like his father (they separated when Gus was 6 months old). When Gus demands things or gets upset over trivial matters, it reminds Toni of how demanding Gus's father was of her. She doesn't see Gus as a toddler who has trouble coping with his emotions – rather, she sees him as a copy of his father who is getting into the same habits of treating her badly and not being reasonable. This affects her responses to Gus. She doesn't know how to diffuse his tantrums, or how to comfort him. When Gus is having a tantrum, Toni is trying to cope with her own distress and fear that she is in the same situation she was with her ex-husband. The effect on Gus is that he is not receiving the emotional help he needs to learn to manage his emotions.

My child is not really feeling the emotion he is showing

This belief interferes with empathy because parents are likely to dismiss the child's emotions because they don't seem real. There is a myth that children pretend to be more upset than they really are to get attention. In reality, children in the toddler years do experience more anger and distress than they generally do in their first year of life. To interpret tantrums or crying as attention-seeking is to short-circuit the process of trying to understand what your child is feeling. But if you consider your child's level of distress from his perspective, then it becomes a weightier matter that is not as easy to dismiss.

My child is not emotionally dependent on me

This belief interferes with empathy because your motivation to understand your child's experiences and emotions is decreased if you feel you don't have much of a role to play in your child's emotional life. In contrast, if you are able to keep in mind that your child is struggling with the changes that toddlerhood brings you are more likely to remain aware of the role you have in helping your child.

Summary

► Toddlerhood is a time of rapid emotional change.

► Your child is developing his own will and striving to master the world around him.

► There is an increase in anger at this age.

► Children are prone to emotional outbursts (or tantrums) when they feel overwhelmed by frustration.

► Parents who empathise and help their child manage their emotions promote emotional health in their child.

From five to twelve years

The primary school years are a time of steady emotional growth. Your child's entry into school is a major transition, and with that comes the development of a peer network, responsibilities and expectations relating to schoolwork and the building up of skills and competencies.

The emotional needs of children aged five to twelve years are:

★ secure attachment

★ ability to communicate with their parents

★ self-esteem

★ feeling competent

★ acceptance by peers

★ a sense of belonging and approval in their family

★ help with emotional regulation when their own strategies aren't working.

SECURE ATTACHMENT

The extent to which a child feels secure in her relationship with her parents tends to remain stable over time. Security is important because it helps the child to trust people, to obtain support from them and to have satisfactory relationships. A child who is securely attached to her parents is ideally placed to enjoy school, participate in events in the community and enjoy her friendships.

The idea of the parent as a secure base continues to be relevant in the primary school years. Instead of running to you crying when she has scraped a knee, the opportunities to give support and comfort can be subtler. Your child may want to talk about what is troubling her at school. There are times when she will feel out of sorts or she will be worried about something. Children who are securely attached are able to express their feelings reasonably well and have a tendency to seek and receive support. Children who are insecurely attached tend to be reluctant to discuss their feelings and problems. The lack of communication seen when a child is insecurely attached is partly her efforts to protect herself. The child is concerned that if she speaks about her feelings she will be vulnerable and something bad may happen. She may fear being ridiculed, it might make her feel worse, or the problem might be embarrassing.

Increasing security of attachment

If you suspect your child is not as secure in her relationship with you as you would like, there are things that you can do to increase security. Changing attachment from insecure to secure is a long process. Here are some tips that may be helpful:

Decide to be a secure base for your child

In practical terms this means making a commitment to help your child when she is upset or needs help. Being a secure base means providing support and encouragement rather than doing everything for your child. Providing emotional support doesn't mean that your child doesn't have to meet certain expectations about behaviour and responsibilities, but it is certainly easier to obtain a child's cooperation in matters of behaviour and responsibilities if she is securely attached. Children who are securely attached are more likely to listen to their parents.

Show it is safe and helpful to share feelings

You may talk to your child about sharing feelings and being open, but the best opportunity arises when your child is actually experiencing emotions. You can take the lead in such a discussion. Your child won't instantly change from being reluctant to discuss her feelings to being open, but rather she may gradually disclose a little bit more on each occasion. If you provide a listening ear, your child may be encouraged to open up a little more, and so it goes.

Use the opportunities you have to give comfort

When your child is upset, she needs comfort from you rather than for you to be dismissive or punitive.

Use real-life opportunities to show support

A child may be upset because her friend has left the school, she is worried about moving to another school or her pet has died. Use these everyday incidents to talk about what has happened and to offer support.

A pattern can be established whereby your child tries to hide her feelings and by the time she loses control and can no longer hide her feelings, she is so upset that she cries in a way that seems out of all proportion to the events. This makes it hard for you to respond sensitively because you are startled by the intensity of the response. If you keep in mind that the emotion was building, but not visible, then you can be more sympathetic and focus on your child's emotional experience and need for support.

Penelope is a nine-year-old girl who has always been quiet. Her mother, Amelia, feels that they are not as close as she would like them to be. Penelope is hard to talk to: she rarely starts conversations, tends to give one-word answers, and often says 'I don't know' in response to Amelia's questions. This worries Amelia – she wants to be close to her daughter and she isn't sure why they have so much trouble communicating. So Amelia makes a concerted effort to improve communication. She starts to spend time alone with Penelope regularly, they walk the dog together every evening, and she makes a special effort to talk to Penelope. At first it feels awkward, but after a while Penelope starts to open up and talk more. With the regular space she is given to talk, and with her mother seemingly interested in all her comments, Penelope slowly finds a way to communicate more with her mother. At first she talks about everyday things – what happened at school, what she would like to do on the holidays. But as she gets more comfortable, she is also able to talk about deeper issues. A few years later, when she is worried about starting high school, she is able to have honest talks with her mother and receive the reassurance she needs.

Patience

Be patient with your child. If you were convinced that someone would react to you a certain way, how long would it take you to be convinced otherwise? And what kind of different experience would you need to have to convince you? An insecurely attached child is convinced she will not receive support. When you go out of your way to be supportive in the face of her distress (for example, saying to the child 'What's the matter? Do you want to talk about it?' in a kind voice) your child may not know how to react, and may be reluctant to expose herself. Understandably, you may feel discouraged and may give up trying to provide support if your child doesn't seem to want it. However, every interaction is an opportunity to show that you do care about how your child is feeling and that you are there to offer support.

Slowly over time your child is likely to venture out, to take risks and perhaps disclose why she is upset or come to you when she is feeling sad or angry, instead of withdrawing. It is important to be as consistent as possible in your support. You can imagine that if your child comes to you (after much reluctance) and then does not feel supported, it will deter her from trying again. However, children do very much want to speak to their parents and to receive support, so there is a natural tendency for parent–child relationships to right themselves, even after difficulties.

COMMUNICATION

Children are in a different position to adults with regard to communication. Adults often have a number of people they can talk to, while children's main source of support and communication is their parents. Children need to be able to talk to their parents or another trusted adult. Communication involves dialogue, a conversation, turn-taking. What can be done to encourage communication?

Creating the opportunity for communication

Time spent together is the basic precondition necessary for communication to occur. This means time without the television on (people tend not to talk much to each other when watching television), and without computer games being played.

Creating more time in your day is a very difficult task and can be hard to sustain. One way to make it easier to create opportunities for conversation is to integrate them into your daily routine. Some ways you might accomplish this are: the family sitting down for dinner; walking the dog together; sitting down on the child's bed for ten minutes when you are tucking her in; or talking in the car on the way to and from school.

Spending time together won't always lead to conversation. Some children are quiet and tend not to talk much. That is fine. The goal is not to change your child's personality, but rather to help her to communicate in her own way. You can encourage a quiet child by starting conversations.

SELF-ESTEEM

Self-esteem is the extent to which someone feels they are a good and worthwhile person. Children's self-esteem is related to their understanding of who they are and what they can do. Self-esteem (or the self-concept) has a number of parts to it: how good the child feels she is at physical skills, schoolwork, in a special area or talent, as well as how worthwhile she feels overall.

You can help your child to develop competencies and self-esteem by encouraging involvement in a range of activities so that your child can find what she enjoys and so build a range of skills. Some children excel in a particular field, while many children don't excel in a single area, but rather feel competent participating in a range of activities.

Parents also play a large role in their child's self-esteem by their daily interactions with the child. These things help to build a child's self-esteem:

★ Treat your child with kindness and consideration. The child is likely to conclude she is a worthwhile person because she is treated as such by her parents.

★ Give your child opportunities to do tasks and show her competence. Encourage her to do the dishes, make her bed and help around the house generally.

★ Praise her for her achievements, kindness and helpfulness. Notice when your child does something good and take the time to comment on it.

★ Encourage your child to express her views, try new things and experience new adventures. This helps your child to feel she is competent and able to manage things, and that her view is important.

Be aware that these things can reduce a child's self-esteem:

★ criticism – constant fault-finding with the child

★ ridicule of the child

★ not helping your child to gain skills and competencies appropriate for her age. If the child is overly dependent on others, she is likely to feel less capable than other children.

FEELING COMPETENT

Children need to feel competent at tasks required of them such as schoolwork, or playing sport. Involvement in community activities such as the local basketball team can give children the opportunity to be good at a range of different things. Involvement in a number of groups is also helpful because your child will not be reliant upon a single group for acceptance. If there is a difficult patch with friends at school, your child has a separate group of friends (in which things are hopefully running more smoothly). Feeling competent may come from many activities – a child may be good at chess, or knitting, or doing elaborate block constructions. Maybe she is the fastest runner on the block or can zoom around on her bike.

Children increasingly compare themselves to their peers and develop a more objective idea of how their talents and achievements measure up against those of others, instead of just being content with mum and dad's praise.

Children of this age are looking to adults for role models and to gain meaning from the activities they do. A child may conclude that she is good at fixing machines like her dad or good at running like her aunt. This helps her to form pictures in her mind about how she is developing and how her future might look.

Justin is an eleven-year-old boy who has always struggled with his schoolwork. He has been diagnosed with a learning disorder. His father, Peter, had high expectations for his son, and is disappointed that Justin cannot seem to keep up with his peers at school. For a few years, his father stayed in the background when it came to school tasks and homework, because he knew he would just end up criticising Justin and making him feel worse. A few times he had tried to help, and he could tell by the look on Justin's face that he felt crushed by Peter's comments (even though he didn't think he was being particularly harsh).

Then it occurred to Peter that he could go out of his way to help Justin feel better about his learning. So Peter started expressing an interest in what Justin was doing at school. He was careful to focus on the positives and he would do some exercises with Justin (like maths and spelling) that were easy enough for him to do confidently. Peter praised him, and showed he was pleased with his performance. Then he slowly made the work a bit harder, and was sure he was on hand to explain things carefully and not be critical. After a few months, Peter has been impressed by how much more enthusiastic Justin is about his schoolwork. It has also brought them closer together. Peter thinks that because he is supportive and not critical when it comes to his schoolwork, Justin trusts him more and is more likely to come to him when he has problems, because he experiences his father as a patient and supportive parent.

ACCEPTANCE BY PEERS

To be emotionally healthy, children need to be accepted by their peers. Children vary in their popularity; some have a wide range of friends, others only a small group. But a child needs to have at least some friends, otherwise the child feels lonely and this can lead to emotional problems. In the context of peer relationships, children learn about social interactions, how to make friends, how to keep friends, how to resolve conflict and how to play cooperatively. Peer relationships are an important source of the child's emotional development in the primary school years. At this stage, supportive friendships are a thing of the future, tending to emerge in adolescence. However, peer relationships are an important component of your child's life, especially because she spends most of her time at school. A child who doesn't have friends at school is emotionally isolated for most of the time. This can make the child feel bad about herself, sad and lonely.

There is evidence that the level of security in attachment influences the type of relationships a child will make with her peers. Children who are securely attached believe that they are worthy of care and expect others to treat them well. Similarly, securely attached children have a healthy interest in other people and expect people to be generally trustworthy.

In a secure attachment relationship, a child learns that her feelings are okay (even feelings such as sadness and anger) and that she will get support. Her experience of being nurtured, supported and accepted is something that she can bring to her relationships with peers. She has a template of how to interact with people, how to support them.

A child with an insecure attachment will be feeling uncertain about whether others will like her. She is probably going to be anxious to gain approval, but may also denigrate other people and not trust their intentions. Children with insecure attachment are more likely to be bullied or to be bullies themselves because the experiences they have had are less supportive than children who are securely attached.

Your child's main peer group is within the school setting. It is normal for children to go through phases of peer difficulties and this does not mean that she is insecurely attached. Having good communication with your child will help you to know what is going on so that you can intervene at school level if need be, and support and help your child deal with painful peer interactions.

A SENSE OF BELONGING AND APPROVAL

Despite spending a lot of their time in school, and establishing interests and friendships outside of the home, family and what happens within the family remains a powerful influence on children's emotional health.

Children need to feel they belong in their family. Spending time having fun, talking and sharing experiences, all help children to feel part of the family. Parents can help to ensure that children feel welcome and approved of. Of course, there are times when you won't approve of your child's behaviour, and you need to make that clear. Make sure that you communicate your approval to your child when you are happy with her.

Parenting styles

Meeting your child's emotional needs is a part of the broader context of parenting. Different parenting styles have been identified and each has a particular influence on children.

Authoritative parenting

This occurs when parents set clear expectations of the child's behaviour but at the same time are responsive to the child's views, emotions and needs. These parents explain to the child the reason for rules, avoid punishment, show praise and warmth and try to establish give and take in the parent–child relationship. Authoritative parenting is related to the highest emotional and social wellbeing in children.

Authoritarian parenting

Authoritarian parents also have clear expectations for their child's behaviour, however the emphasis is on the parents' authority and expectation to be obeyed. These parents tend not to consider the child's opinions and feelings but rather are concerned with the child's obedience. Children who are raised using the authoritarian parenting style can be resentful and have problems with their emotional regulation.

Permissive parenting

Permissive parents see their role as their child's friend rather than guide. Permissive parents allow the child freedom to choose her activities, and provide minimal monitoring. Permissive parents do not set clear boundaries or expectations about the child's behaviour. Permissive parenting is related to childhood depression and anxiety problems and to less social competence and lower achievement compared with other parenting styles.

Neglectful parenting

This occurs when parents are not responsive to the child, and have no expectations about their child's behaviour. Neglectful parents lack involvement with their child. These children are at risk for psychological difficulties and delinquency.

HELP WITH EMOTIONAL REGULATION

Between the ages of five and twelve years, children acquire new skills to cope with their emotions. They also develop a better understanding of their own feelings and those of others. In contrast to the preschool age, when children need a lot of help to regulate their emotions, children at this age are able to manage their own feelings most of the time. At times, your child will require assistance. For example, if your child is particularly tired or stressed about new events, she may need help to manage her emotions.

HOMEWORK AND SCHOOL ACHIEVEMENT

One issue that can arise as a difficulty during the primary school years is homework. If you want your child to do well at school, you need to set up the emotional and physical conditions to make that possible.

Children need support in the learning process to help them with these challenges:

A sense of achievement

We tend to enjoy the things we can do well. Likewise, for a child to enjoy learning, she needs to have a sense of achievement. If a child is struggling with schoolwork, then some easier work can be set that is still challenging, but allows your child to show her ability. Parents who praise their child for their effort and results they achieve are sending a message that schoolwork is important.

Coping with errors

The learning process involves making mistakes (if no mistakes are made, then the person already knows it all!). But there is a natural tendency to not want to make mistakes. This can prevent children from trying new things, and so can reduce their engagement in the learning process (they are so focused on getting the right answer, they don't think more broadly or creatively). You can help your child by encouraging her to try different ways of solving the problem and by your responses to your child's errors.

Routine

School achievement depends in part on having good routines. Children can find it hard to organise themselves or to be consistent. You can help your child by negotiating a routine and then helping your child to follow it. It may be helpful for you to write out the routine and put it up somewhere both you and your child can refer to it on a daily basis.

Parental involvement and interest

Children are more likely to do well academically if their parents are interested in their schoolwork and involved with helping them. Try to set aside some time each day to help with homework, or at least be available if your child feels she would like your help.

Summary

► Children of primary school age continue to develop ways of managing their emotions and broadening their experiences outside the family.

► Emotional health is still largely influenced by the interactions your child has within the home.

► There is much that you can do to help your child develop emotional health.

PART THREE

EMOTIONAL DIFFICULTIES

Emotional disorders in childhood

It is widely known that adults can suffer anxiety and depression. It is less well known that children, even very young ones, can suffer from these disorders too. Many children experience transient problems in their emotional development or with regulating their emotions. Other children, however, experience emotional disorders such as anxiety or depression (or both) and these disorders influence their development and compromise their wellbeing.

ANXIETY DISORDERS

Anxiety disorders are more common than depression. Children who suffer from anxiety disorders are more likely to suffer depression than those without anxiety disorders. Of course, some anxiety in children is normal. They may be scared of the dark, of spiders or of needles. Anxiety is only considered a disorder if it persists, distresses a child, or compromises a child's functioning (for example, the child won't attend school or participate in other activities). Anxiety need not be high to interfere with a child's functioning. There is evidence that anxiety can interfere with children's school achievement.

There is a range of anxiety disorders that affect children:

Specific phobias

This is the most common type of anxiety disorder. A child is intensely fearful of a particular situation or object, for example, heights, spiders, dogs, needles or closed spaces like lifts. The child experiences intense fear when confronted with the object, or when he anticipates confronting the object or situation.

Separation anxiety disorder

A child suffering from separation anxiety disorder is excessively fearful about losing his attachment figure(s), most typically his parents. He will tend to be clingy and may be reluctant or refuse to be separated from the parent to the point that he resists attending school, avoids school camps and staying overnight at friends' houses. The child's fear is that he will be permanently separated from his parent, possibly by the death of his parent or himself, by his parent leaving and not coming back, or by being kidnapped or becoming lost. Some children are fearful to the extent that they become distressed if they are not in the same room as their parent. For instance, if the parent goes to hang up the washing, the child will insist on following them. At night the separation anxiety may become more pronounced and the child may be distressed about being separated and resist going to sleep unless a parent is with him. If the child is separated he is likely to be very distressed, and may experience physical symptoms such as stomach aches or vomiting.

Some separation anxiety is normal

Every child is concerned at some stage or another about becoming separated from his parents. Parents are his source of security. A child will typically start to exhibit separation anxiety in his first year of life, which is normal. Children usually become less concerned about separation as they get older so that by the time they attend kindergarten and school, they are able to separate easily.

Dealing with separation anxiety

1. *Recognise your child's distress.* You leave the room for a moment and your child cries and runs after you. Or your child is tucked up warm in bed, but if you leave his room, he cries and calls after you, no matter how much you reassure him that you are still in the house. These behaviours may not seem rational. You might think that your child's distress isn't really as extreme as it looks. Be assured that the distress is real. Only by taking your child's feelings seriously can you help him with his emotions.

2. *Respond consistently.* Secure attachment is based on your child knowing from experience that you are there for him when he needs you. When your child is experiencing separation anxiety, he is worried that he may lose his parent permanently. This anxiety can be terrifying for a child. In order for your child to feel secure, he needs you to respond to him consistently. Parents sometimes worry that they are encouraging dependence if they respond to their child, so instead they let him cry. This confirms the child's fear that he can't have access to his parent when he needs them.

3. *Encourage independence.* Independence cannot be forced, it can only be encouraged. The more you try to force your child to be independent, the more your child may cling to you because he is likely to feel pushed away (and this makes him feel unsafe). You can encourage your child to move a little beyond his comfort zone. Encouragement is given by saying to your child 'I think you will be

fine for a few minutes without me, but if you need me I will be back.' This takes the battle out of the interaction as you are no longer trying to wrest yourself away from your child, but you are making it clear that you will be there when you are needed. Often this can increase your child's sense of security and he no longer needs to be next to you all the time.

Generalised anxiety disorder

Children with generalised anxiety disorder worry excessively about everyday issues such as their family, friends, about their performance or schoolwork not being good enough, or global events like natural disasters and wars. Children with this anxiety disorder are often worried and have difficulty controlling their worry.

Social phobia

This involves excessive discomfort about interacting with peers (and of course can include worries about interacting with adults). The child is scared of being embarrassed or negatively judged by other people. They may avoid interacting with others, or experience distress when they do interact.

Obsessive compulsive disorder

This involves obsessions (repetitive, intrusive thoughts) and compulsions. For example, a child may worry that something terrible will happen to his family unless he touches the objects on his bed in a certain order. Children may be preoccupied about handwashing because of fear of germs.

Panic disorder

This involves episodes of feelings of panic accompanied by physical symptoms like nausea and light-headedness. These episodes have no known trigger. While it is far more common in adults, children may also experience panic disorder.

THE RISK FACTORS FOR ANXIETY

The risk factors for anxiety are:

★ a family history of anxiety disorder

★ shyness

★ certain parenting practices (focusing on danger; critical and unsupportive interactions).

Family history of anxiety disorder

A family history of anxiety disorders increases a child's risk of developing the disorder. This may be due to a genetic predisposition, as well as environmental influences. People with anxiety disorders think differently from those without the disorder: they focus on danger, they interpret neutral cues as indicating danger (for example, the sound of a car backfiring may be wrongly perceived as gunfire); they overestimate the likelihood of negative events happening; they focus on physiological symptoms of anxiety (racing heart, sweatiness, butterflies in the stomach); and they don't feel able to cope with everyday situations that may arise.

Shyness

Children differ in their temperament. Some are outgoing and confident, others are withdrawn and shy and tend to be fearful of new situations and people. This latter group is more likely to experience anxiety.

Parenting practices

A range of parenting behaviours is related to childhood anxiety. This includes parenting that is critical, lacking in warmth, over-controlling, overprotective and that focuses on danger.

It is not clear why criticism would be related to anxiety in children but presumably it makes children feel insecure. When we are criticised we feel that something is wrong (with us, or the situation we are in). When we criticise, we show disapproval. To feel secure, a child needs his parent's approval.

Likewise, a lack of warmth in interactions with his parents may increase a child's insecurity with the result that the child is more prone to feeling anxious about all sorts of things.

Over-controlling behaviour is when parents are intrusive and interfere with the child's actions and choices. This may result in the child lacking self-confidence because he is not given the opportunity to try out things for himself. Overprotection is when a parent goes too far in trying to protect the child from experiences.

Overprotection may be the result of the child's initial anxiety: the parent sees the child is anxious and so tries to help him by keeping the child away from the situation. However, avoiding the object of your fear is likely to increase your fear. For example, children who don't go to school because of anxiety are likely to find it harder to go back the longer they stay away. When a parent helps their child to avoid something, the message given to the child is that it is dangerous and should be avoided, which serves to reinforce the child's original anxiety.

Helping to reduce your child's anxiety

There are a number of ways you can help your child with anxiety. Some useful strategies include:

★ *being aware of what you say to your child.* It is important not to dwell on the things that might go wrong (sometimes parents might talk at length about such things in an effort to prepare their child) as this is likely to increase your child's anxiety and make him more likely to interpret events as threatening. Your child is more likely to be relaxed if you talk in a positive and reassuring way, and model a non-anxious attitude.

★ *helping your child to problem-solve.* It can be helpful for you to discuss with your child different ways he could make himself feel better. For example, remembering times that he has coped well; considering who he might go to for help and support when you are not around; having calming thoughts, distracting himself from worries rather than ruminating on them, and so on. This is likely to help your child gain a feeling of competence in handling anxiety and worries.

★ *supporting your child.* It is important for your child to feel that you are willing and able to support him. This means that you show with your words and actions that you care about your child's experiences, are willing to talk to him, and that you are someone he can turn to for comfort and advice.

Some anxiety is normal

Everyone experiences some level of anxiety from time to time. If you've woken up late and you are rushing, you may well be feeling anxious, wondering if you will make it on time. Or you might have had a medical test and you are worried about the result. These are everyday events that might stir anxiety. Likewise, your child might be anxious about starting school, doing a presentation, performing at a dance concert, or having a new experience like going to school camp for the first time. So when your child is feeling anxious, you might acknowledge it by saying, 'Are you feeling a bit worried?' and then reassuring him that he will be fine: 'Many children worry when they go on their first camp, but you'll be fine.'

Be confident in your child's ability to cope

When your child is feeling anxious, he might wonder about his ability to cope. You need to inspire confidence in your child. If you are looking worried and uncertain about whether he should go ahead with something, this will fuel the child's anxiety. From the time your child was a baby, he took cues from you about what was safe and what was dangerous. Parents communicate this by their tone of voice, by their facial expression. If you are looking very worried but saying 'you'll be fine', your child is likely to believe your nonverbal signs.

Helping your child problem-solve

There are two ways to problem-solve: by trying to fix the situation, or by finding ways of coping with the feelings caused by the situation. Depending on the circumstances, either or both of these solutions may be appropriate. Sometimes children are anxious because of what is going on around them, for example they are bullied at school. In this case, it would be appropriate to not only find a way to deal with their anxiety, but also to find a way to stop the bullying. The school should be contacted. Your child may be given a list of things to do if he is bullied (speak to a particular teacher, go to the library, find the principal, etc). With a specific action plan, your child should feel empowered and more able to deal with the situation.

Dealing with the feelings of anxiety involves two main strategies: physical relaxation and changing thinking patterns. Anxiety often results in physical tension and symptoms such as dizziness, pins and needles, a feeling of light-headedness or nausea. Learning to do deep muscle relaxation, listening to soothing music and having a peaceful environment can all help to reduce anxiety. Challenging and replacing negative thoughts is also important. If your child tells himself that something terrible will happen, then it is no wonder his level of anxiety is high. You can be helpful by identifying your child's thinking then trying to shift the focus to the positive side of the situation, rather than the dangers and the negative things that might happen.

Providing support

Parental reassurance is important to children, and so is the manner in which it is given. Parents who are anxious themselves may unwittingly communicate that there is something to be anxious about. Parents can sometimes be too painfully aware of the uncertainties of their lives. After all, none of us really knows what tomorrow will bring. This uncertainty, if communicated to the child, can fuel a child's anxiety. For example, if a child fears that his parent will be killed in a car accident, it is not helpful for the parent to agree that there is that chance (of course the chance exists, but stating this to the child will probably lead to the child overestimating the risk, and to a heightened state of anxiety). Too much information can increase rather than decrease anxiety. Of course, you know there are risks and dangers, but for the most part you can keep this to yourself and reassure your child that all is well. You have the responsibility of addressing these issues; your child is too young for the emotional burden of worrying about dangers and risks in his life.

Fluctuating anxiety

The progress of an anxiety disorder tends to fluctuate. There are periods where the child is highly anxious, and other times when anxiety reduces. Children who have anxiety disorders are more likely to experience them in adolescence and adulthood. It can seriously undermine their quality of life, so seeking professional treatment is important if anxiety seems to be impacting on your child's life or causing him distress.

CHILDHOOD DEPRESSION

Another childhood emotional disorder is depression. There is evidence that the rate of childhood depression is rising. Children can have major depressive disorder, dysthymic disorder and, more rarely, bipolar disorder (formerly known as manic depression). Childhood depression is believed to be the same disorder as adult depression, but the symptoms can vary. Sadness is a prominent feature of adult depression, whereas children who are depressed may be irritable and angry rather than sad. The child may fly off the handle, overreact to minor events, frown and look sullen. They may appear sad, withdrawn, lethargic, lack interest in activities and have low self-esteem. They may have problems concentrating or making decisions, feel guilty about all sorts of things and talk about death. They may say they want to kill themselves, or that they want to die or be killed.

The risk factors for depression are:

★ a family history of depressive disorders

★ stressful life events

★ harsh and punitive parenting.

Family history

It is believed there is a genetic component to depression so that in families where a parent or other relative has depression, a child is more likely to develop depression (but of course this is not inevitable).

Stressful life events

Research has shown that children who suffer depression have more stressful life events including conflict with peers, family difficulties, poverty, bullying and so on.

Harsh parenting

Children who have depression tend to receive parenting that is harsher, more punitive, less communicative and less empathic than children who don't suffer depression. Of course, parenting a child who has a mood problem is a stress in itself. Children with depression have a tendency to isolate themselves – they may spend long periods of time in their room, be unresponsive or look blank or sad. This withdrawn and flat behaviour can discourage parents from communicating (they may give up after a while) and this further compounds their child's isolation. Children who are depressed often don't know why and may even struggle to state their feelings, especially if the child has been depressed for a while. They may not be aware of how their mood differs from a 'normal' mood.

Seek help

Childhood depression can come and go, or it can be chronic. It is important to seek help from your general practitioner, a psychologist or psychiatrist if you suspect your child may be depressed. Children with depression experience a lot of distress, and it often affects their ability to learn at school, friendships, family relationships, and it can affect their behaviour. There is evidence that the negative effects of childhood depression can last for many years and can be seen in adulthood. A child who has depression is more likely to also experience it again during his teenage years and adulthood.

DYSTHYMIC DISORDER

Dysthymic disorder involves a child being sad or irritable for most of the day, for more than half of the time, for at least one year. On average, dysthymic disorder in children lasts for about four years. This means a child may be unwell for more than half his life by the age of seven for example. There is evidence that children as young as two or three years can have this disorder. It is a serious disorder that affects a child's quality of life, his academic and social progress, and puts him at high risk of ongoing psychiatric disorders. Eighty percent of children with dysthymic disorder go on to develop major depression. Children can have 'double depression', that is, both major depressive disorder and dysthymic disorder. The risk of suicide, substance abuse and school dropout are all increased with depressive disorders.

Commonly a child with dysthymic disorder appears to be in a continual bad mood. He may scowl, cry easily, be upset easily, have emotional outbursts, get angry over minor incidents and seem generally unhappy. Because of its chronic nature, dysthymic disorder may go undiagnosed. The chronic irritability may be attributed to the child's personality. Children with dysthymic disorder may have trouble falling asleep, or problems with eating (overeating or undereating), low energy, trouble concentrating or making decisions, or feeling hopeless. These children often have behaviour problems. They tend to be uncooperative, talk back to their parents and may find it hard to do schoolwork or chores. They may complain that no-one loves them. They might say they wish they were dead or that they want to kill themselves or want others to kill them.

Jemima is a 6-year-old only child. Her mother described Jemima as a difficult baby, and she suspected something was wrong from the beginning. Jemima had trouble settling down and she cried a lot. As a toddler she had severe tantrums, pulling her hair, head banging and biting. Sometimes she would scream for hours. Her mother tried many different things, and took her to many professionals, but the problems continued. Now Jemima is an irritable child who has a blank expression on her face most of the time. She has low self-esteem (she tells her mother she is hopeless), fights with other children, and has many tantrums each day. Jemima is suffering from dysthymic disorder. The time it began is unclear, but the disorder has emerged against a background of emotional regulation problems that go back to infancy.

BIPOLAR DISORDER

Bipolar disorder in children is rare. Children with bipolar disorder alternate between times of depression (as explained above) and times of mania. Mania symptoms include extreme overactivity or irritability, inflated self-esteem, less need for sleep than usual, and racing thoughts.

ANXIETY/MOOD PROBLEMS AND DAILY LIFE

It is important to consider what is going on in a child's life rather than just focusing on the mood or anxiety problem as if there is no connection between the two. Having said that, it may not be possible to identify anything in the child's life that appears to be concerning him. In that case you might ask yourself these questions:

★ How can I help my child to feel better?

★ Do I need to spend more time with my child, or have special times together, or just listen to my child more?

If you suspect your child may have an emotional disorder, it is important to seek professional assistance. This can be obtained through your general practitioner, a maternal and child health nurse, a psychologist, a psychiatrist, or child mental health services.

Summary

▶ Children may experience emotional disorders, including depression and anxiety, at a young age.

▶ It is important to seek professional assistance if you are concerned about your child's emotional development. It is easier to help the child in the early stages, rather than waiting until the disorder has been present for a long time.

Common difficulties and how to alleviate them

While some children develop anxiety or depressive disorders, more commonly children experience everyday difficulties with their emotions. Everyday emotional problems can reduce a child's wellbeing and her ability to cope and can be a real challenge for parents. Children's everyday emotional problems can:

★ improve with time

★ worsen with time

★ stay the same.

It's very hard to predict the likely outcome for an individual child. Parents who try to understand their child's everyday emotional issues, and to deal with them constructively, give the child the best chance of leaving the problem behind.

Signs of emotional problems

These are some signs that your child may be experiencing emotional problems.

Birth to one year

★ excessive crying and is unable to be soothed

★ wears a blank expression, does not smile or look at people.

One to four years

★ severe tantrums during which your child smashes objects, pulls her own hair, bites or hits herself or bangs her head

★ extremely passive (not interested in toys and games)

★ cruel to people or animals.

Five to twelve years

★ frequent tantrums	★ frequent anger
★ often tearful	★ looks sad, does not smile often
★ socially withdrawn	★ not interested in much
★ cruel to people or animals	★ worried a lot of the time.

Some of the difficulties that children may experience include low self-esteem, insecure attachment, constant whingeing and lack of cooperation.

LOW SELF–ESTEEM

Oliver is a nine-year-old boy with low self-esteem. He underestimates his abilities and often feels his performance isn't what it should be. He believes his schoolwork isn't good enough and he expects that children won't like him. When a friend invited him to join the local basketball team, Oliver was sure he'd be no good at it and declined the offer. Feedback that would be expected to bolster his self-esteem may not affect how he sees himself. When Oliver does get things right (like receiving an art award at school) he puts it down to chance rather than his own ability.

What Oliver's parents could do to help

Oliver's parents are concerned about his low self-esteem, and puzzled as well because they see that Oliver is good at many things, but he just doesn't seem to believe that he is. There are a few things that Oliver's parents could do to help.

Avoid criticism

On first reading this suggestion, many parents would say, 'I don't criticise my child.' But if they think about it carefully, it is often the case that they do not mean to criticise, but that their child interprets their comments as critical. Children with low self-esteem are very sensitive to potential negative evaluations. It can be hard to appreciate just how sensitive they are. So a well-meaning parent may be offering suggestions on improving performance, but all the child hears is 'you've done it wrong'.

Give frequent and genuine positive feedback

You can actively look for opportunities to give positive feedback. Feedback needs to be genuine. If you think your child hasn't done something well, then don't say you think she has. Rather try to find some aspect of her performance or effort that you are truly impressed with, and tell her so. It can be hard to stay positive because your child may retort, 'You don't mean that.' But if you reiterate calmly and with conviction that you think your child is good at something, she will be listening. Even if it doesn't look like your child is taking it on board, if she hears the message repeatedly, it is likely to have some impact.

Don't qualify praise

When praising your child, don't contaminate the praise by saying something at the end that might be taken as criticism. If there is corrective feedback you have to give, do it separately from the positive comments, otherwise your child will focus only on the negative feedback, and the impact of your positive statements will be lost.

✓ ✓ Positive and specific

'I really liked how you shot that goal – you looked really determined.'

Oliver has something solid here. By being specific the parent is showing that he or she was paying attention. Specific feedback also has the role of providing evidence to Oliver that he is good. Oliver can check his parent's comments against his own recollection of the match. ('Yes, I did score that goal', Oliver would think.)

✓ Positive but vague

'I really liked your performance at basketball today.'

Certainly this is positive, but Oliver could easily dismiss this comment, not because he doesn't want to believe that he is good. On the contrary, he is probably desperate to feel better about himself, but it is hard for him to believe that he is a good player. His parent's statement is so general, that when he compares the comment with his own beliefs about his playing ability, he could think, 'I know I'm not a good player so what they are saying isn't true.' The vague comment doesn't give him anything solid to grasp. In contrast, a child with high self-esteem would more easily benefit from a general positive comment because he could link it with specific memories and beliefs he has about himself. He might think, 'Yes, I am a good basketball player because I remember when I scored five goals for the team', or 'My coach told me last week I was doing really well'.

✗ Positive statement with negative qualification

'I really liked how you shot that goal. It just shows you can do it if you are determined. Maybe if you were determined at the beginning of the match, you would have scored when you had that opportunity in the first five minutes.'

You can see how with the addition of the last sentence, Oliver might be left with the feeling he should have done better and that what he did was not good enough! The parent starts with the right intention, but they are focused on trying to improve the child's performance rather than giving praise for his achievement.

Choose words carefully

There are times when parents need to give suggestions or feedback that is aimed at correcting something that the child is doing. Do this as gently as possible for the child with low self-esteem because she is easily hurt, even when you have no such intention. Try to say things in a positive way if possible. There's a huge difference between 'Please put away your dishes' and 'Put those dishes away, don't be so lazy.' Try to focus on what your child should be doing rather than what she should not be doing.

Be aware of your tone of voice and facial expression. Your child is sensitive to the nonverbal behaviours that accompany messages from you. Even if your words are calm and reasonable, if you look disgusted or angry this contaminates the message you are sending.

THE INSECURELY ATTACHED CHILD

Zoe is a seven-year-old girl who has developed an insecure attachment with her parents. When Zoe was younger her parents were stressed (due to illness and unemployment) and were unable to care for her in a supportive and responsive way. Often her parents were too stressed with their own problems to notice what Zoe needed emotionally from them. They let her cry for long periods of time, didn't comfort her, and were unresponsive to her bids for attention. As a result, Zoe does not feel confident that they will be there for her if she needs them. Zoe finds it hard to share her feelings; she withdraws into herself, and is grumpy and distant when things go wrong for her. Her style of coping with problems is to try to depend on herself. Even when things are stressful and she can't make herself feel better, she is still unable to reach out to her parents for help. Zoe behaves well when she is in a reasonable mood, but at other times, she has tantrums and crying episodes.

Zoe's parents

Zoe's parents feel distant from her. They wish it were otherwise, but they feel they can't quite connect with their daughter – she seems to be in a world of her own. Often she does annoying things, and is irritable and grumpy (then her parents start to feel grumpy with her). She hardly ever shows affection, and seems serious-minded for a seven-year-old. They've tried talking to her about her tantrums, but she doesn't seem to be listening. When they try to speak to her about the problems she is having at school, she rebuffs them and withdraws (and seems angry they tried). In some ways they have given up on having a better relationship with Zoe and suspect maybe it's just her personality. Zoe reminds her mother of a grandparent who was difficult to get along with, and so she wonders if Zoe's problems are genetic.

Zoe's difficulties from an emotional development perspective

Zoe is avoidantly attached to her parents. This means that she feels insecure about whether her parents will be there for her when she needs them. She feels uncomfortable talking to her parents about her feelings, so she avoids doing so. Zoe thinks she should try to depend on herself because she is not sure she would get help if she asked for it. Zoe is defensive. When her parents try to get her to open up, she wants to stay in control of her feelings and so she pushes them away. She doesn't believe she would feel better if she spoke to them, in fact, she believes she may feel worse – maybe they would be upset with her, or even laugh at her.

For Zoe to build a more secure attachment relationship with her parents, she needs to have different experiences with her parents, including those that show her it is safe to talk about feelings. She also needs to consistently receive soothing and comfort when she is upset.

What could Zoe's parents do to improve the situation?

Zoe's parents could improve the situation by consistently providing her with a different emotional experience with them. To do this, her parents need to have certain beliefs:

1. Zoe's behavioural problems and reluctance to seek support have developed because of her experiences (as opposed to reflecting a difficult personality).

If Zoe's parents believe that her difficulties result from actual experiences, they are more likely to be motivated to support her. Otherwise, they may blame her for her problems, or at least think she is partially responsible for her problems. If her parents believe she has tantrums and is emotionally distant because it is part of her personality, they will feel powerless to change it to any significant extent, and so their motivation to do things differently will be compromised.

2. Zoe needs to have the experience of sharing her feelings and have it end up positively for her.

If Zoe's parents realise the importance of her feeling able to discuss her negative emotions and experiences, they will look for opportunities to encourage her to speak, and find ways to show her support.

What you believe and how you interpret your child's behaviour influences your behaviour towards your child, which in turn has a big impact on her emotional state and development. This is true of most social interactions: if we think someone is being unreasonable or trying to frustrate us, we are likely keep away from them or retaliate. On the other hand, if we think someone is trying to get along with us, we are likely to be supportive and understanding.

Parenting behaviour that would help Zoe

Zoe needs to feel supported when she is upset. For Zoe to be convinced that her parents are really there for her and that speaking to them will make her feel better, she needs not just their words (many of us are not convinced by words alone), but action. Zoe needs support and comfort when she is upset. This point cannot be stressed enough: for children to be securely attached they need emotional support when they are upset. Many parents are able to speak to their children about emotions when their child is calm and feeling fine. But as soon as the tantrum or crying or yelling starts, parents may withdraw from the child or cut off emotional communication. They may demand the child calms down, instead of helping the child to calm down. This reinforces to the child that she is on her own emotionally.

Tips for Zoe's parents when she is upset

★ Believe she is genuinely upset (without this, it is hard to provide genuine comfort).

★ Be supportive.

★ Help her cope with her distress.

★ Persevere and continue to try to be supportive (even though she might initially seem unresponsive).

When she is upset, Zoe needs support and help with regulating her emotions. But at other times, there are also things her parents could do to improve the security of their relationship.

Tips for Zoe's parents when she is not upset

★ *Find reasons to make small talk.* For example, Zoe is at the kitchen table, being silent as usual. Her mother might say, 'Look at the sky, aren't the clouds pretty?', 'What are you going to do at school today?' or 'Where do you think we should go on the weekend?' For Zoe to talk more openly about her feelings, she first needs experiences of talking about everyday things.

★ *Smile and show positive feelings towards Zoe.* Every time her parents smile at her or show her affection or make a nice comment to her, they are showing her that they like her, approve of her, care for her and are interested in her. Zoe needs to believe these things before she can feel comfortable about sharing her feelings.

★ *Find positive aspects of Zoe's behaviour to praise.* Even the smallest things can be used as a reason to say something positive to her.

★ *Try to integrate Zoe into the family.* If she won't make conversation, find ways to engage her.

★ *Spend time together with her doing activities she enjoys.*

A key challenge is for Zoe's parents to be positive towards her even if she is not positive towards them.

Beliefs that are likely to maintain the difficulties

★ Zoe is not really upset, she is attention seeking.

★ She doesn't appreciate what we are trying to do for her.

★ Her personality is causing the problems.

★ She has 'bad' genes (as proven by her resemblance to her father, mother, uncle, or other disliked member of the family).

★ She might just grow out of it on her own.

★ She'll change her mind and approach us.

The challenges of increasing security

The main challenges for parents who are trying to increase the security of the relationship are to provide support, be consistent and persevere.

Providing support at the time of your child's need

The timing of support is critical. It is relatively easy to be positive when your child is smiling and calm. It is much harder to provide emotional support when your child is crying and yelling.

Consistency

When you are feeling calm, you may be able to provide emotional support. But it may be that when you are under pressure or stress, you revert to old habits. For real and lasting change to occur there needs to be consistency in dealing with your child and her emotions. Because your child may become upset without prior warning (and often at the most inconvenient time!) it can be hard for you to be thoughtful about your response.

Perseverance

Many parents are able to try something new for a few days, but when their child doesn't seem to change, they find it hard to maintain the required effort. In Zoe's case, it took her years to develop an insecure (avoidant) attachment relationship. Increasing her security will not happen overnight.

The negative cycle

You might find yourself in this position: your child is negative (arguing, crying, not cooperating), and so are you (criticising, ignoring, yelling). Neither you nor your child is happy in your interactions, and the interactions feed each other. How do you go about shifting the dynamic?

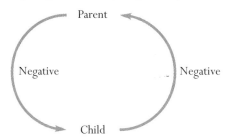

First step

Because adults are more able to change and have better reasoning skills than children, they are in a better position to break the cycle. If you decide to be positive, despite your child's negativity, she is likely to respond. This may not happen immediately, so initially you may feel you are working hard, yet your child is still negative. Don't be put off. Persevere and be patient.

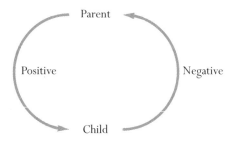

Resolution

In most cases, it will not take too long for your child to respond. At first it may be only occasionally, but soon she will feel better (because she is not having negative interactions with you) and this will be reflected in the way she responds to you. Once there is a positive cycle, it tends to perpetuate itself.

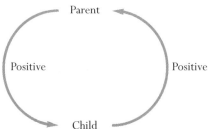

THE WHINGEING CHILD

Thomas is a four-year-old child who whinges incessantly. Everything upsets him. He cries, has tantrums and is difficult to calm down.

Thomas's parents

Thomas's parents are understandably exasperated. No matter what they do, Thomas seems unhappy. Sometimes it seems that if they pay him attention and try to soothe him, it just makes it worse. Interactions are negative with lots of yelling and ignoring, resulting in a miserable time together.

Thomas's emotional development

Thomas's tantrums and prolonged grumpy mood show that he is overwhelmed with his negative feelings. Thomas being upset so often is a sign that he is not managing his emotions as well as he might. The more quickly his parents try to help him regulate his emotions and improve his mood, the better chance there is that Thomas will grow up emotionally healthy.

Providing emotional support and soothing to Thomas so that he is less upset less often does not mean that his parents approve of his behaviour. Instead they are acknowledging that he is truly upset by trying to communicate their understanding and care for him, and implementing strategies to help calm him.

Obstacles to improvement

There are a number of pitfalls his parents may fall into (or may have already fallen into) that could make the situation worse, or prevent it from improving.

Seeing the interactions as a battle

When a child is behaving in a way that causes disruption and a lot of noise, it is easy for you to interpret the commotion as directed against you. If you see the behaviour as designed to upset or undermine you, you will take a defensive position (you protecting yourself against your child). This defensiveness may be shown by emotionally cutting off your child while she is behaving in an undesirable way, or it may involve criticising or punishing the child to bring her back into line. None of these helps the child to cope better or to calm down.

Not seeing the emotions

When children's behaviour is annoying or frustrating, parents tend to focus on the behaviour. The behaviour takes centre stage, and the child's emotions recede into the background. Thomas's parents might be convinced he is badly behaved and not see the role that his emotions are playing. They try to make Thomas 'behave better', and don't address the underlying emotions that are actually fuelling his behaviour.

Seeing emotions as a key part of the problem, but not offering help

His parents might see that he does indeed get very upset, and they might see the link between his feelings and his behaviour. But it might stop there because they could think that Thomas needs to learn to handle his own feelings, and that the best way to teach him how to deal with his feelings is to show him that he won't be 'rewarded' for being upset. As such, they don't comfort him when he is having a tantrum, but rather they let him get over the emotional turmoil himself, which can take quite some time.

Reasoning rather than soothing

Thomas's parents might be active in trying to help him manage his emotions, but their approach might be too rational. Instead of soothing him by giving him a hug, telling him they understand how he feels, and trying to 'sit' with his feelings, they try to talk him out of his feelings. They might have an adult-type conversation (which even an adult may not find soothing) along the lines of 'There is no need to be angry because …' or 'Instead of acting the way you did, if you had been nice … this wouldn't have happened … and you wouldn't have gotten upset'. Although this may be true, Thomas is likely to feel criticised rather than understood. Part of soothing your child certainly involves using words to show her you understand or to find a way of helping her to feel better, but conversation can easily become too rational and not contain the emotional soothing that your child needs.

Beliefs that are likely to prevent improvement

★ Thomas is not really upset, he is just attention-seeking.

★ He is trying to control me by his bad behaviour.

★ He does this on purpose to try to upset me.

What might Thomas's parents do to improve the situation?

Try to empathise with Thomas

To provide comfort and soothing that Thomas needs, his parents must empathise with him. They need to try to understand what is going on from Thomas's perspective (which could be very different from their perspective). To empathise they need to believe that all that screaming and crying really reflects how Thomas feels. He is very upset.

Help him regulate his emotions

Parents who empathise and can put themselves in their child's shoes will find it much easier to offer the comfort that he needs to calm down. Trying to calm him when they suspect the whole thing is a performance will be very hard. The parents' efforts at soothing may come across as fake and insincere. Our facial expressions, tone of voice and body language quite easily give away how we really feel. If Thomas's parents think he is being manipulative or just plain 'naughty', they will feel annoyed or even furious, especially if this pattern of behaviour has been going on for some time. When parents feel annoyed or furious, neither emotional state will allow them to soothe the child.

Step-by-step improvements

Thomas's current whingeing state took a long time to develop. Hopefully, it can be changed in a much shorter time, but it will not happen overnight. It is about step-by-step improvements. Each time he gets upset, or is about to get upset, is a chance for his parents to improve things.

The main challenges for parents trying to decrease whingeing

1. *Being positive towards your negative child.* It requires considerable emotional energy to stay positive towards

someone who expresses a lot of negativity. It is relatively easy to either tune out from your child's mood and negative responses or to be negative yourself ('you are always whingeing' or 'nothing makes you happy'). Parents who show more warmth (by tone of voice, affection) tend to have children who whinge less.

2. *Seeing whingeing as a result of mood rather than personality.* When do adults whinge? When they are feeling down or frustrated. When people are happy they don't whinge. Your child is the same. So you can be sure that when your child is whingeing, she is not feeling content. It doesn't matter what the 'objective reality' of the situation is. It may seem from a distance that everything is just fine, but if your child doesn't feel that things are fine, she will be influenced by how she feels, not by the 'objective' perspective.

Thoughts to help you stay calm and focused

★ She is only a child.

★ She needs me to help her with her emotions.

★ She is behaving like this because she is emotionally immature.

★ When she gets overwhelmed by her emotions, this is the behaviour that results.

★ She is having trouble getting through the day (or the evening routine, or morning routine) in a happy way.

★ Her ability to reason and control herself is much less than an adult's.

If you feel calmer, you are much more likely to say the things and perform the actions that actually soothe your child.

SOOTHING A CHILD

There are three steps involved in soothing a child:

1. Listen

2. Show that you care, and

3. Solve the problem that is upsetting your child.

Listen

Listening is not always easy. Often people might think they are listening, when they are not. They assume they know what the person will say, so they are constructing their comeback or making judgements about the situation that favour their viewpoint, rather than trying to find out about the other person's viewpoint.

A number of activities are involved in listening to your child:

★ Let your child speak without interrupting or finishing her sentence for her.

★ Try to concentrate on what your child is saying rather than making negative evaluations about her. For example, your child doesn't want to share. You may be listening to your child complain and thinking 'You never want to share, you just don't know how to think of anyone but yourself.' It may be true that your child needs to learn how to share, but having these negative thoughts about your child makes it less likely that you will actually hear her concerns.

★ Try to accept that your child's view and experience are valid. Her view is not necessarily convenient or 'rational'. It may not fit with your view of the situation, but it is her experience. In order to help your child find a meaningful resolution, you need to understand her point of view. If you discount her view as not real or not accurate, then the starting point for dealing with the issue cuts out her perspective.

★ Show that you are listening. Being listened to can be a great relief. You can probably think of times when you've experienced difficulties or misfortune and you had someone to listen to you. The person listening may not have been able to do anything about the situation, but it was probably a comfort to have someone with whom to share the experience.

Tips to show you are listening

★ *Repeat what your child says.* Your child says, 'Jack always gets more chances to see his friends.' You say 'You think he gets more chances than you.' You may disagree with your child's statement, but it is important to give your child the chance to state her opinion. By repeating the comment back to the child, you are not agreeing that Jack gets more chances, but rather you are acknowledging that your child feels as though he does. This is likely to make your child feel somewhat calmer because now she has someone listening to her. If you cut your child off and say, 'That's not true, you went to visit your friend last week and Jack hasn't seen anyone for two weeks', your child would probably argue. Then it would become a tussle about who is right and who can provide more evidence about their perspective. Really, the point is not about objective truth, but rather how your child is feeling at this point in time.

> ★ *Show that you hear the underlying message or feeling.* You might say, 'It sounds like you think this is unfair.' Your child may not have said that, but from her tone of voice, or the content of her speech, it may seem to be the underlying message she is trying to communicate.

A parent who listens is likely to have a different kind of conversation than one who doesn't. If your child is heard, she is more likely to listen to you, and a conversation might ensue about the issue. She may need reassurance, a reminder or plans for the future from you. None of this would happen if you were not listening to begin with.

Impediments to listening

★ *Thinking you know what your child will say.* Sometimes you might not really listen to your child because you think you know what your child is going to say. Sometimes you will be able to anticipate what your child wants to say, but at other times you won't know. Give her the chance to tell you. What has upset your child in a particular situation is not always obvious and it may well be different to what upset her in a previous situation.

★ *Deciding that your child is not being rational.* You might think 'There is nothing wrong about this situation. There is nothing for my child to be upset about.' If you have reached this conclusion, there's no reason to listen to your child. However, if you take your child's feelings seriously, you show that you are interested in her perspective. Your child's perspective is influenced by her maturity, her mood and her own individuality. Try not to assume that one perspective is right and another is wrong. Hearing your child is the first step to having a meaningful conversation or finding a solution to the situation. Otherwise, the child is likely to be upset not only about the situation, but also about the fact she is not being listened to.

Show that you care

After you have listened to your child and shown her that you hear what she is saying, show that you care. It does not mean that you agree with her behaviour, or even with her view of the situation, only that you accept that this is how she is experiencing the situation, and that you care about how she feels. You need to feel reasonably sympathetic, otherwise your words will sound hollow.

Your care is communicated in a number of ways:

★ how you look – is your facial expression tense and impartial or open and concerned?

★ what you say

★ your actions, e.g. asking a sibling to stop teasing.

Solve the problem

After listening and showing your child you care about her feelings, the next step is to help your child with the situation. Broadly speaking, there are two types of problem-solving: managing feelings or managing the situation (or you can do both).

Coping with feelings

The first thing you can do is to help your child feel better, perhaps by giving her a hug or distracting her to another activity. Sometimes, there is nothing that can be done about the situation – the pet has died, or the child must go to school even though she is anxious. The challenge is how you manage the feelings related to those events. Making a memorial for a pet, or just talking can provide comfort to a grieving child. A child who is anxious about going to school needs to go nevertheless. Again, the challenge is to manage and reduce the anxiety. Showing confidence in your child and her teachers (that they will look after the child), focusing on the positive aspects of school, being clear about the routine, and so on, can all help a child to feel less anxious.

Changing the situation

Sometimes something can be done about the situation. If your child is upset about bullying, then something needs to be done to address that behaviour. It would not be adequate to just help her to somehow cope with the negative feelings of victimisation. Rather, action is required. You would need to visit the school, enlist the cooperation of school staff and carefully monitor events. In this case, the action you take would give your child the message that neither you nor the school community thinks it is acceptable for her to have to put up with that kind of treatment. As a result, she would most probably feel more confident and less defeated by her experiences.

Paying attention to the situation that is upsetting the child is an important part of helping her with her feelings. There are certain events that children should not be exposed to. Situations including verbal abuse, name-calling, teasing, bullying, physical or emotional attacks are upsetting for children and adults alike. Parents need to respond to this type of situation in order to help the child emotionally.

Melanie is an eleven-year-old girl who lives with her parents and her fifteen-year-old brother Jason. Her parents seek help for her 'anger management' problems. She has explosions of anger, she swears, screams and even throws things around. She usually has at least one outburst a day. When family interactions are spoken of, it is clear that her brother Jason often upsets her. He takes her diary and runs around the house with it (reading the interesting bits aloud), he pushes her out of the way if she is standing too close to him, or is in his way, and he calls her names and yells at her. This pattern of behaviour has become so entrenched that it is taken for granted. While Melanie does experience a lot of anger, her anger cannot be understood without considering the context in which she is experiencing her anger.

It is important to note that your child's emotional experience cannot be understood without considering the interactions she has with other people, and the general environment she is exposed to.

Soothing in a nutshell

1. Listen.
2. Show you care about your child's feelings and perspective.
3. Help her to problem-solve or deal with her feelings by:
   ★ offering a hug
   ★ distraction
   ★ offering another activity that is enjoyable
   ★ planning for the future

★ giving reassurance

★ staying calm, and helping her calm down.

LACK OF COOPERATION

A child's lack of cooperation is most commonly interpreted as 'bad' behaviour. It is vital to understand that emotions often underpin a child's non-cooperation.

For your child to function in society, at school, and later in the workplace, she needs to know how to cooperate with other people, how to take instruction and to perform tasks she may not feel like doing. Setting appropriate tasks for your child given her age and ability will help her to acquire skills that will help her succeed in life. Some of the objectives of cooperation are:

★ helping your child to learn to consider others

★ teaching your child that she is helpful and valuable to others

★ teaching self-discipline – just because you don't feel like doing something doesn't mean that you don't do it!

Things you can do to increase cooperation

★ *Be cooperative towards your child* as a role model. Find opportunities to cooperate with her activities, to help her out, and so on. If you are not a cooperative person yourself, it will be hard for your child to be so.

★ *Listen to your child's concerns* when she is not being cooperative. There may be some legitimacy to her complaint.

★ *Choose your timing.* If you ask your child to help dry the dishes just as her favourite television show is starting, chances are she will say no. Some parents feel that their child should listen to them regardless of what is on television, but this is denying a human characteristic. Even adults don't like to be interrupted during their favourite activity.

★ *Give advance warning*. Rather than springing a request out of the blue, try to think ahead to what you require your child to do and let her know ahead of time.

★ *Negotiate the timing of what needs to occur* as far as possible. 'I need you to clean your room today. Do you want to do it before or after dinner?'

★ *Be consistent.* If the rules and expectations change often, your child is likely to feel resentful and not understand what is expected of her.

★ *Give some choice* (if appropriate). 'I need help tidying the house today. Do you want to sweep the floor or load the dishwasher?'

Things to avoid when seeking cooperation

★ *Increasing threats.* If you threaten to take away your child's favourite activity or toy if they don't comply with a request, your child might cooperate and this may be a solution in the short term. However, too much reliance on threats makes your child feel that she is being forced to do something that she doesn't really want to do. It's much better to appeal to your child's sense of empathy than to threaten her into doing things, which will eventually lead to resentment.

★ *Inconsistency.* Your child will do certain tasks more easily if they become habit. If expectations change often, children will not know what is expected of them and struggle with the changing demands made on them.

Most parents would like their children to *want* to be helpful and to be motivated by the benefits to others and themselves if they cooperate. Ideally, parents need to find ways to make cooperation a positive rather than negative experience.

Your child is less likely to cooperate if:

★ there is tension or conflict in the parent–child relationship. If you are fighting with someone for most of the time, you are unlikely to want to cooperate when a request is made. On the other hand, if you get along with someone, there tends to be a natural tendency to want to please the person

★ your child is on the receiving end of yelling, fighting and criticism

★ your child's emotional needs are not met

★ you take an approach that is too hard-line, as your child will feel bossed around and will be tempted to rebel. Too casual an approach will mean she will not have a clear understanding of whether she actually has to cooperate, or whether it's an option.

Summary

▶ Virtually all children will at some time or another show signs of everyday emotional difficulties.

▶ You are best able to help your child move positively through this time if you consider:

   1. your child's emotional needs and stage of development

   2. what your child needs from you to help her get back on track emotionally

   3. the importance of being emotionally supportive.

▶ Children who experience emotional difficulties can be set on a different path to ensure their emotional health into the longer term, but it can take a lot of thought and effort on the part of their parents.

Author's notes

Page 12, **'Not all academic problems relate to emotional problems, but research does show that emotional problems (for example, even mild anxiety) interfere with children's learning and academic achievement'**: Ialongo, N, Edelsohn, G, Werthamer-Larsson, L, Crockett, L & Kellam, S, 'The significance of self-reported anxious symptoms in first grade children: prediction to anxious symptoms and adaptive functioning in fifth grade', *Journal of Child Psychology and Psychiatry,* 1995; 36, pp. 427–437.

Page 24, **'Usually children have one or two primary attachments, most commonly with their parents'**: Bowlby, J, *Attachment and Loss,* vol. 1, Random House, Sydney, 1997.

Page 33, **'Insecurely attached children showed less joy as they aged, compared to securely attached children'**: Kochanska, G, 'Emotional development in children with different attachment histories: the first three years', *Child Development*, 72, pp. 474–490, 2001.

Page 33, **'Four types of attachment have been identified. These can be divided into two groups: secure and insecure. The three insecure types can be further divided into…anxious..'**: Ainsworth, M, Blehar, M, Waters, E & Wall, S, *Patterns of attachment*, Hillsdale NJ: Erlbaum, 1978. See also Main, M & Solomon, J, 'Procedures for identifying infants as disorganized/disoriented during the Ainsworth Strange Situation' in Greenberg, M, Cicchetti D & Cummings, M (eds.), *Attachment in the preschool years: theory, research, and intervention*, pp. 121–160, University of Chicago Press, 1993.

Page 35, **'Secure attachment promotes resilience in children'**: Sroufe, L, 'From infant attachment to promotion of adolescent autonomy: prospective, longitudinal data on the role of parents in development' in Borkowski, JG & Ramey, SL (eds.), *Parenting and the child's world*, Erlbaum, New Jersey, 2002, pp. 187–202.

Page 36, **'Research around the world has shown the types of parenting that lead to secure and insecure attachment'**: Posada,

J, Jacobs, A, Richmond, M, Carbonell, O, Alzate, G, Bustamante, M & Quiceno, J, 'Maternal caregiving and infant security in two cultures', *Developmental Psychology*, 2002, 38, pp.67–78.

Page 37, **'One study found that securely and insecurely attached children were physically held just as much by their mothers':** Grossmann, K, 'Avoidance as a communicative strategy in attachment relationships', paper presented at the fourth world congress of the World Association of Infant Psychiatry and Allied Disciplines, Lugano, Switzerland, 1989.

Page 38, **'In one study, the sequence of interactions between a parent and child was examined in detail':** Cohn, J & Tronick, E, 'Specificity of infants' responses to mothers' affective behaviour', *Journal of the American Academy of Child and Adolescent Psychiatry*, 1989, 28, pp. 242–248.

Page 39, **'Securely attached adults tend to have relationships that are satisfying … disclose their feelings':** Cassidy, J, 'Adult romantic attachment: a developmental perspective on individual differences', *Review of General Psychology*, 2000; 4, pp.111–131.

Page 41, **'For example, in the Strange Situation (a method of assessing attachment style), children who are avoidantly attached tend to look unconcerned and aloof':** Pederson, D, & Moran, G, 'Expressions of the attachment relationship outside of the Strange Situation', *Child Development*, 1996; 67, pp.915–927.

Page 43, **'These children tend not to seek … They tend to be critical of others':** Bretherton, I, 'The origins of attachment theory: John Bowlby and Mary Ainsworth', *Developmental Psychology*, 1992; 28, pp.759–775.

Page 48, **'Because quality of attachment is dependent on parenting, if parenting changes then the quality of attachment can change':** Vondra, J, Shaw, D Chrisman, J. Swearinger, E, Cohen, L, & Owens, E, 'Attachment stability and emotional and behavioural regulation from infancy to preschool age', *Development and Psychopathology*, 2001; 13, pp.13–33.

Page 50, **'Some research has found … and therefore the risk of insecure attachment increased':** Bakermans-Kranenburg, M, van IJzendoorn, M, & Juffer, F, 'Less is more: meta-analyses of sensitivity and attachment interventions in early childhood', *Psychological Bulletin*, 2003; 129, pp.195–215.

Page 56, **'Babies experience emotions from the time they are born (possibly even before birth), including distress and contentment':** Camras, L, 'Expressive development and basic emotions', *Cognition and Emotion,* 1992; 6, pp. 269–284.

Page 57, **'Babies are affected ... enjoy the interaction':** Cohn, J & Tronick, E, 'Specificity of infants' responses to mothers' affective behaviour', *Journal of the American Academy of Child and Adolescent Psychiatry*, 1989; 28, pp. 242–248.

Page 60, **'Children whose parents help them with emotional regulation are better able to reach their potential, to have harmonious social relationships, and to experience wellbeing':** Eisenberg, N, Cumberland, A & Spinrad, T, 'Parental socialization of emotion', *Psychological Inquiry*, 1998; 9, pp.241–273.

Page 66, **'A child between twelve and eighteen months ... may offer a tissue or give the person a hug':** Dunn, J, *The beginnings of social understanding,* Harvard University Press, Cambridge, 1988.

Page 66, **'A child who receives empathy as part of their daily care is much more likely to develop empathy towards other people':** Koestner, R, Franz, C & Weinberger, J, 'The family origins of empathic concern: a 26-year longitudinal study', *Journal of Personality and Social Psychology,* 1990, 58, pp. 709–717.

Page 67, **'If a child is angry or upset, there is less chance she will empathise in a particular situation. It is hard to think about other people's feelings if our own feelings are overwhelming us':** Eisenberg, N, Fabes, R, Shepard, S, Murphy B, Jones S & Guthrie I, 'Contemporaneous and longitudinal prediction of children's sympathy from dispositional regulation and emotionality', *Developmental Psychology*, 34, 1998, pp. 910–924.

Page 67, **'The extent to which caregivers help the child to focus on the other person's feelings':** Zahn-Waxler, C & Radke-Yarrow, M, Wagner, E & Chapman, M, 'The origins of empathic concern', *Motivation and Emotion*, 1992; 14, pp. 107–130.

Page 122, **'Research has shown that babies who are attended to quickly and consistently cry less than babies who are not':** Karen, R, *Becoming attached,* Oxford University Press, New Jersey, 1998.

Page 124, **'One study found that parents … responsive to their babies':** Crockenberg, S, 'Infant irritability, mother responsiveness, and social support influences on the security of infant-mother attachment', *Child Development*, 1981, 52, pp. 857–865.

Page 132, **'Children who receive help … security in their relationship with their parents':** Kochanska, G, Murray, K & Harlan, E, 'Effortful control in early childhood: continuity and change, antecedents, and implications for social development', *Developmental Psychology*, 2000; 36, pp. 220–232.

Page 136, **'Broadly speaking, there are three ways you can respond to your child if he is showing negative feelings such as sadness or anger':** Fabes, R, Leonard, S, Kupanoff, K & Martin, C, 'Parental coping with children's negative emotions: relations with children's emotional and social responding', *Child Development*, 2001; 72, pp. 907-920.

Page 160, **'There is evidence that the level of security in attachment influences the type of relationships a child will make with her peers':** Elicker, J, Englund, M & Sroufe, A, 'Predicting peer competence and peer relationships in childhood from early parent–child relationships' in Parke, R & Ladd, G (eds.), *Family-peer relationships: modes of linkage*, Erlbaum, Hillsdale, NJ: 1992.

Page 161, **'Different parenting styles have been identified and each has a particular influence on children':** Darling, N & Steinberg, L, 'Parenting style as context: an integrative model', *Psychological Bulletin*, 1993; 113, pp. 487–496.

Page 168, **'It is widely known … compromise their wellbeing':** Kovacs, M, Obrosky, S, Gatsonis, C & Richards, C, 'First episode major depressive and dysthymic disorder in childhood: clinical and sociodemographic factors in recovery', *Journal of the American Academy of Child and Adolescent Psychiatry*, 1997; 36, pp. 777–784.

Page 168, **'There is evidence that anxiety can interfere with children's school achievement':** Ialongo, N, Edelsohn, G, Werthamer-Larsson, L, Crockett, L & Kellam, S, 'The significance of self-reported anxious symptoms in first grade children: prediction to anxious symptoms and adaptive functioning in fifth grade', *Journal of Child Psychology and Psychiatry*, 1995, 36, pp.427–437.

Other Finch titles of interest

Raising Boys
Why boys are different — and how to help them become happy and well-balanced men
Steve Biddulph
ISBN 0646314 181
Audio: A double-cassette set read by Steve Biddulph
ISBN 1 876451 254

Raising Girls
Why girls are different — and how to help them grow up happy and strong
Gisela Preuschoff
ISBN 1876451 599

Adolescence
A guide for parents
Michael Carr-Gregg and Erin Shale
ISBN 1876451 351

Teen Stages
How to guide the journey to adulthood
Ken & Elizabeth Mellor
ISBN 1876451 386

Lessons from my Child
Parents' experiences of life with a disabled child
Cindy Dowling, Dr Neil Nicoll & Bernadette Thomas
ISBN 1876451548

Starting School
How to help your child be prepared
Sue Berne
ISBN 1 876451 475

A Handbook for Happy Families
A practical and fun-filled guide to managing children's behaviour
Dr John Irvine
ISBN 1 876451 416

Confident Parenting
How to set limits, be considerate and stay in charge
Dr William Doherty
ISBN 1876451 467

Fathering from the Fast Lane
Practical ideas for busy dads
Dr Bruce Robinson
ISBN 1876451 211

Parenting after Separation
Making the most of family changes
Jill Burrett
ISBN 1876451 378

Stepfamily Life
Why it is different — and how to make it work
Margaret Newman
ISBN 1876451 521

Bullybusting
How to help children deal with teasing and bullying
Evelyn Field
ISBN 1876451 041

On Their Own
Boys growing up underfathered
Rex McCann
ISBN 1876451 084

Chasing Ideas
The fun of freeing your child's imagination
Christine Durham
ISBN 1876451 181

ParentCraft
A practical guide to raising children well (2nd edition)
Ken & Elizabeth Mellor
ISBN 1876451 19X

Fear-free Children
Dr Janet Hall
ISBN 1876451 238

Fight-free Families
Dr Janet Hall
ISBN 1876451 22X

The Happy Family
Ken & Elizabeth Mellor
ISBN 1876451 122

For further information on these and all of our titles, visit our website: www.finch.com.au

Index